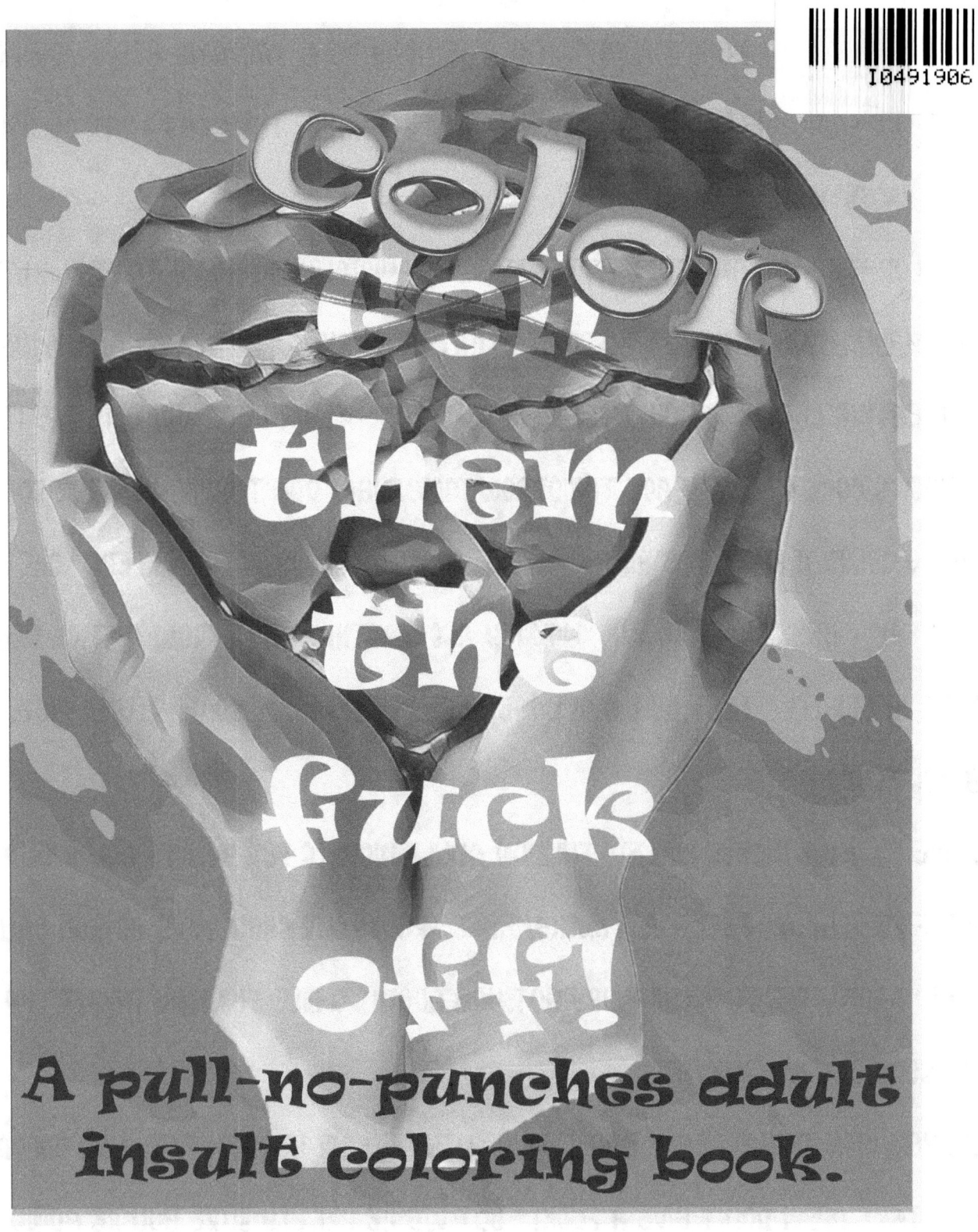

Color them the fuck off!

A pull-no-punches adult insult coloring book.

Cover art and back cover art/ hands-on-Image
by Marek Studzinski from Pixabay

THEY SAY THAT COLORING IS THERAPEUTIC. THEY SAY THAT COLORING HELPS YOU RELAX AND HAS THE SAME EFFECT AS MEDITATION ON THE BRAIN. THEY SAY THAT COLORING REDUCES ANXIETY AND FEAR.

SO IF I COLOR FLOWERS AND CUTE LITTLE FUCKING ANIMALS, I'M GOING TO FEEL BETTER ABOUT MY CHEATING FUCKING BOYFRIEND! THAT COLORING A PICTURE OF A FUCKING BABY GIRAFFE EATING LEAVES IS GOING TO RELEASE THE TENSION I FEEL WHEN I HAVE TO SMILE IN MY BOSS'S COCK SUCKING FACE TOMORROW MORNING! I DON'T FUCKING THINK SO!

I WANT TO COLOR A BIG "FUCK YOU!" I WANT TO COLOR IN BIG BOLD LETTERS "SHE IS A SHIT-LICKER!" "HE'S SUCH A DICK!" "LICK MY ASS-FROTH!" "IF I THROW A STICK WILL YOU FUCK OFF AFTER IT?" THAT WILL MAKE ME FEEL BETTER. NOT SOME STUPID PICTURE OF A DUMB ASS ELEPHANT.

HERE ARE 50, NO PUNCHES PULLED, FULL ON ADULT INSULTS FOR YOU TO COLOR AND MAKE YOURSELF FEEL GOOD! FEEL THE TENSION EASE FROM YOUR SHOULDERS AS YOU CALMLY COLOR IN "DAMN, THE FUCK-UP FAIRY GOT YOU GOOD!" WHILE THINKING ABOUT THAT SPECIAL SOMEONE IN YOUR LIFE.

MAYBE YOU WON'T FIND PEACE AND TRANQUILITY IN YOUR HEART AFTER YOU COLOR IN "YOU MISTAKE ME. I DON'T GIVE A FUCK!" BUT WE'RE PRETTY SURE YOU'RE GOING TO FEEL A WHOLE LOT BETTER!

SO, SIT BACK, RELAX AND

COLOR THEM THE FUCK OFF!

This is _____'s fucking book! Keep your

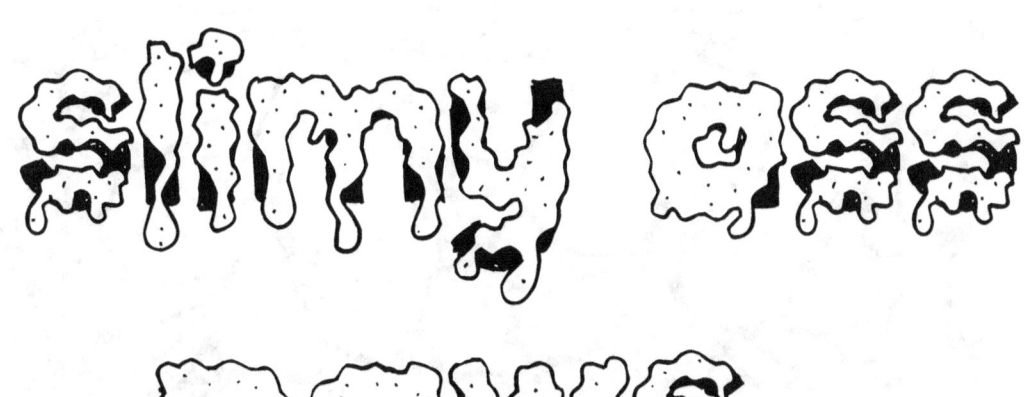

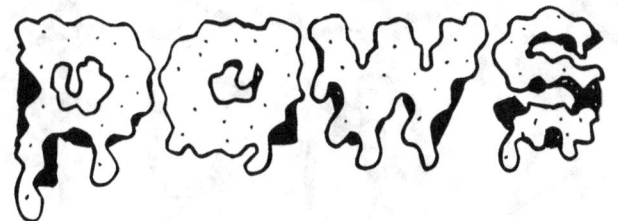

off it!

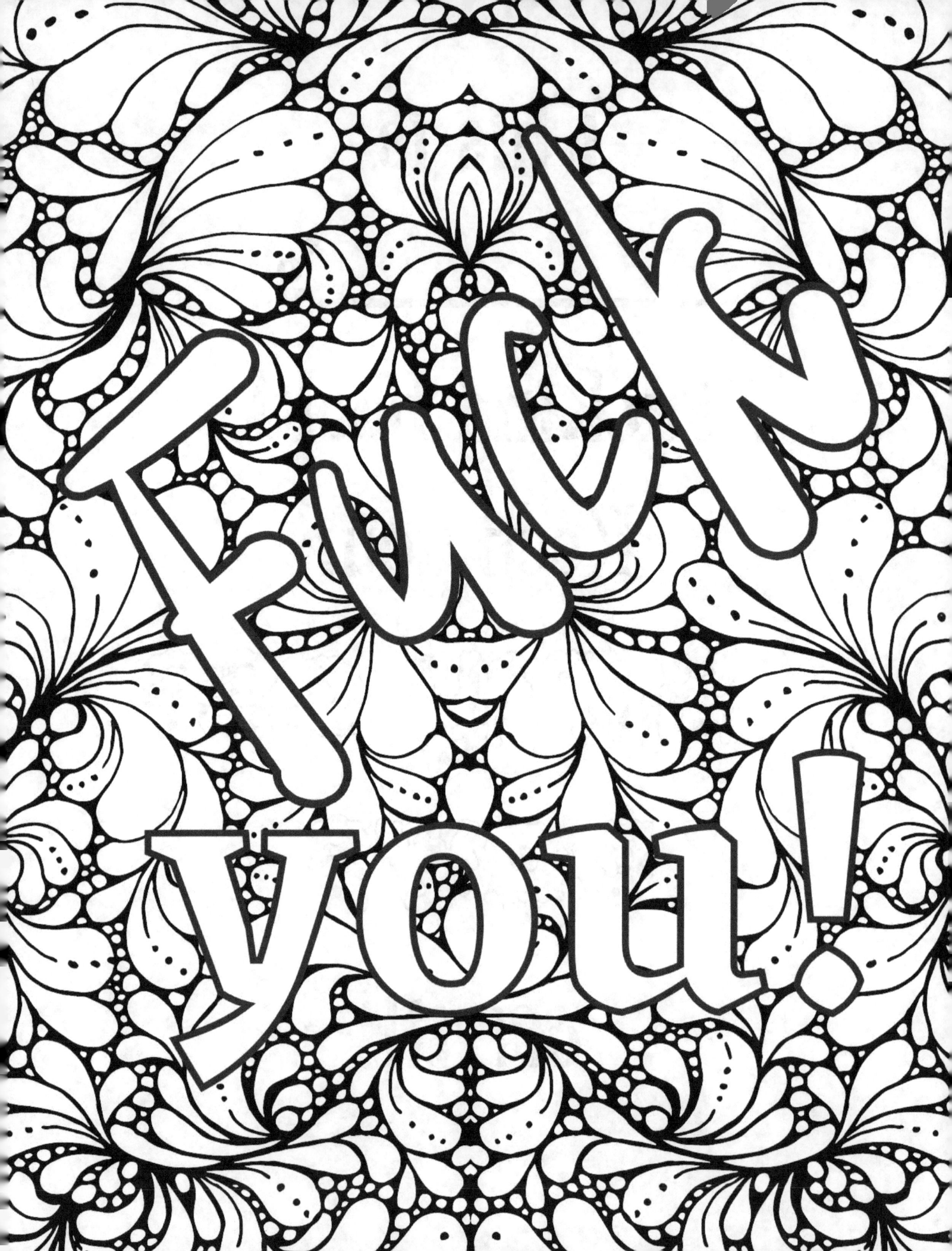

Feel better, yet?

No?!

Then color

the

next

fucking

page!

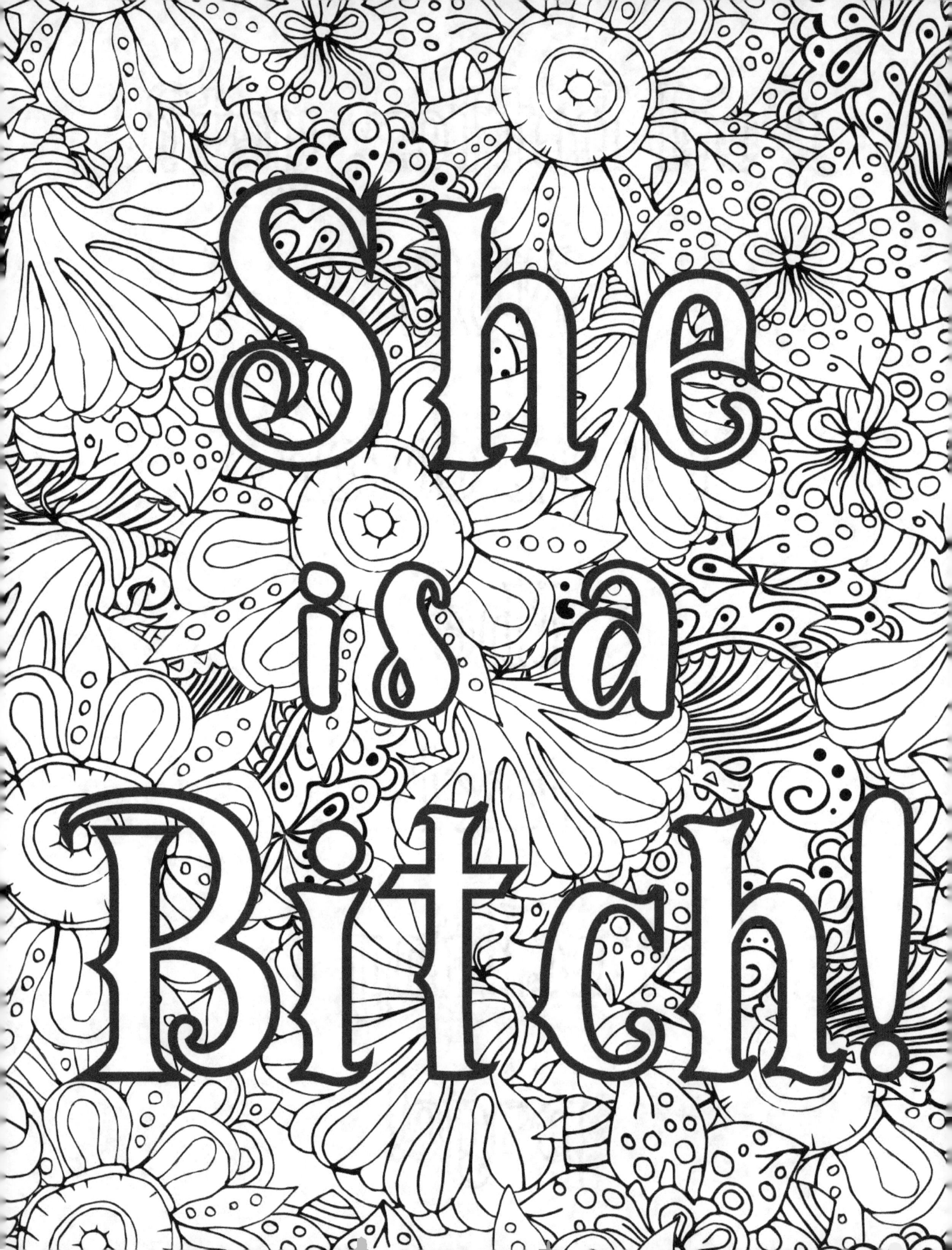

All good now?
No?!
Then get to
coloring
the next
page!

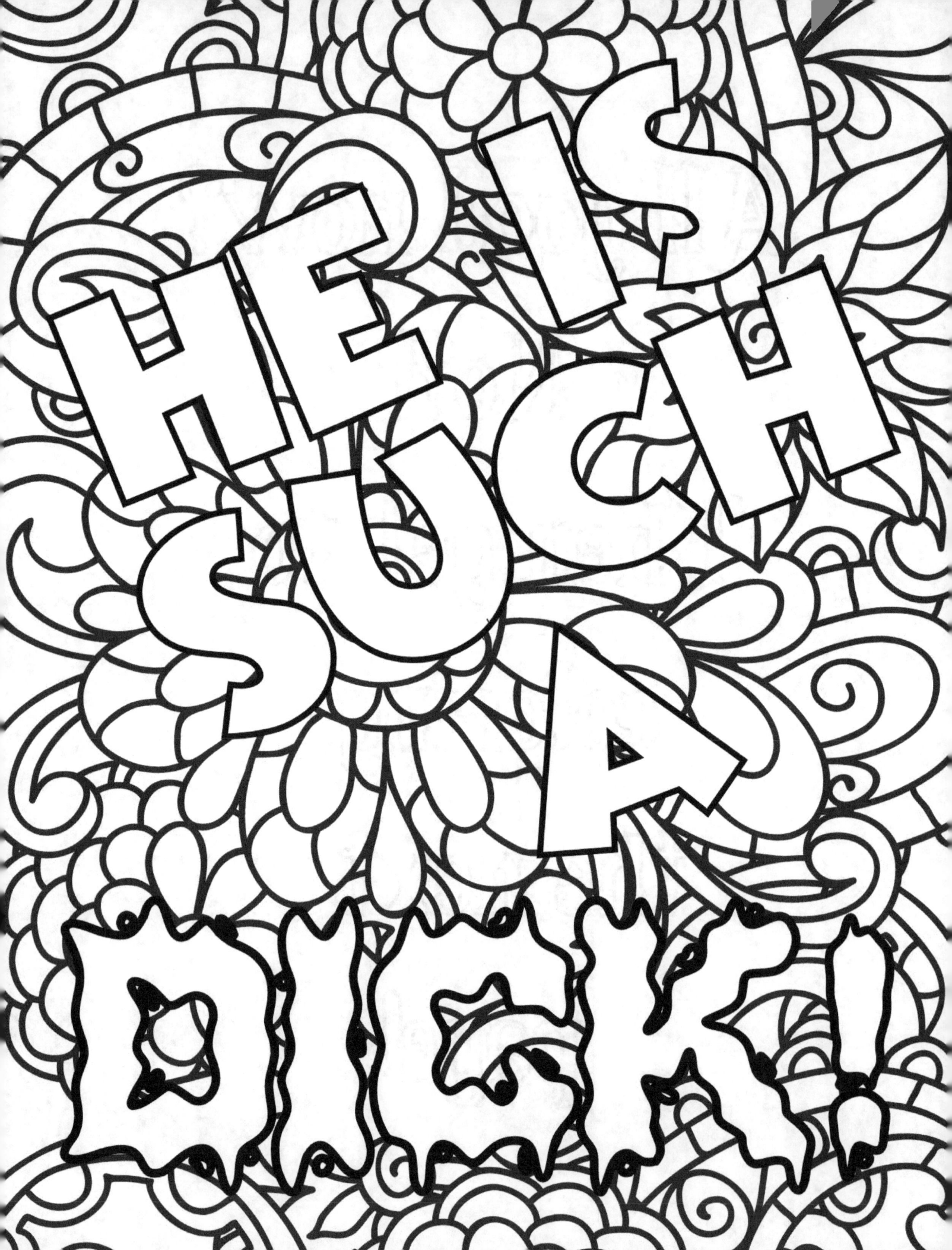

Feeling good?
Not yet?!
Then on to
the
next
tasty
page!

That got you
feeling good?
No?
Then knock some
color onto the
next page!

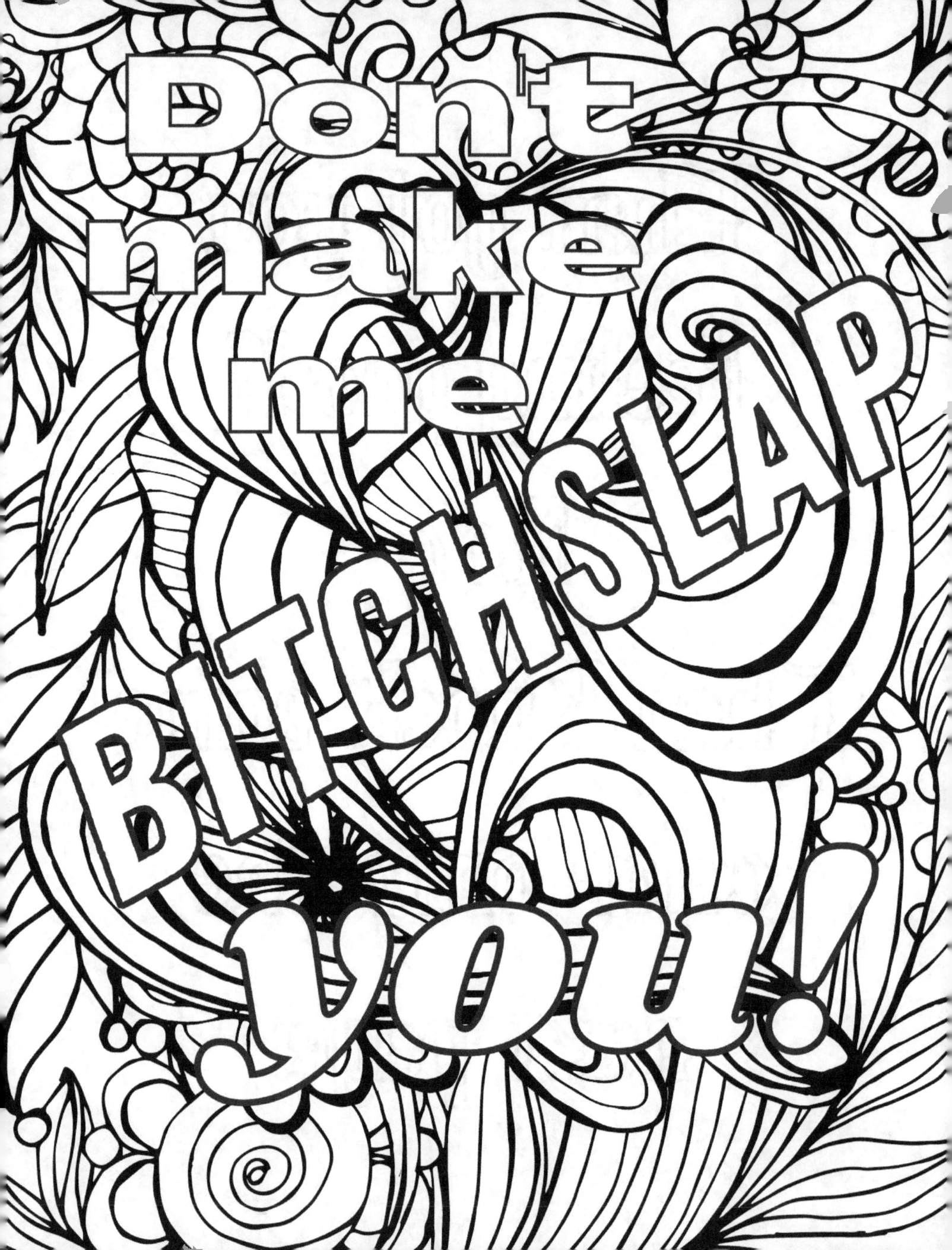

Got your groove back? Not yet? Well then, keep on coloring. This next page is sure to do the trick!

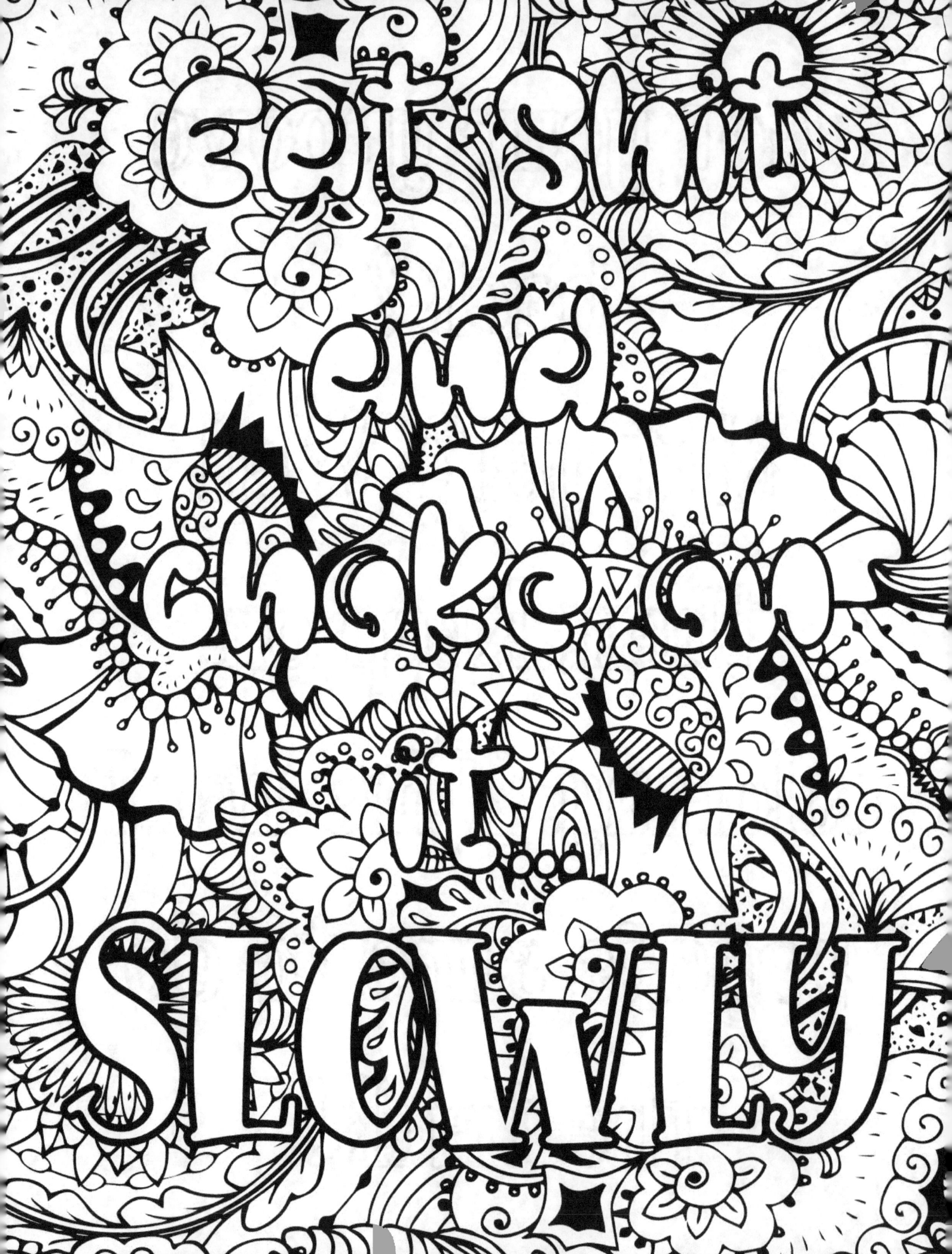

Feel your anger easing away? Still got more? Then coloring this next page is gonna feel goooooood!

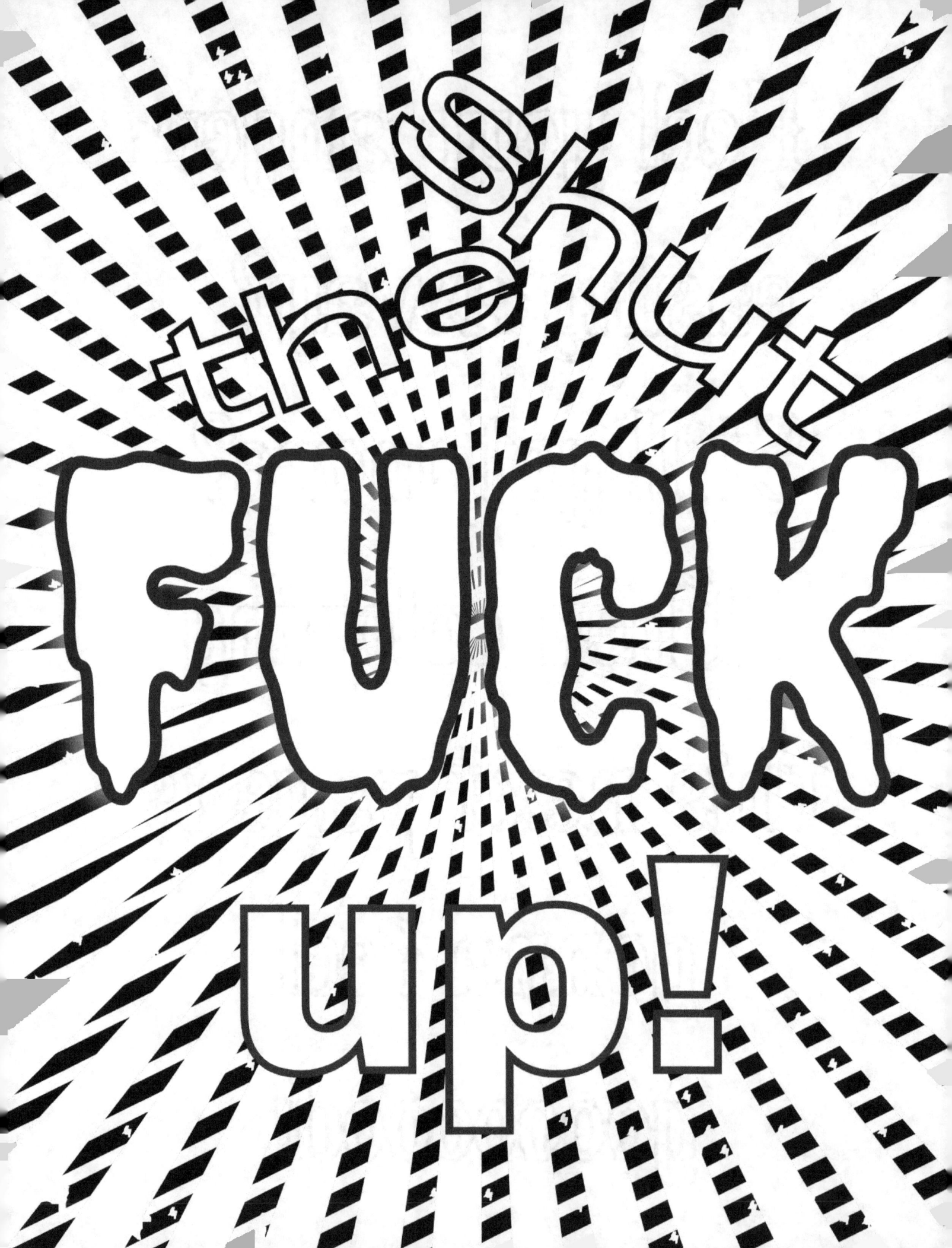

Feels nice,
right?
This next one
is an oldie but
a goody.
Enjoy!

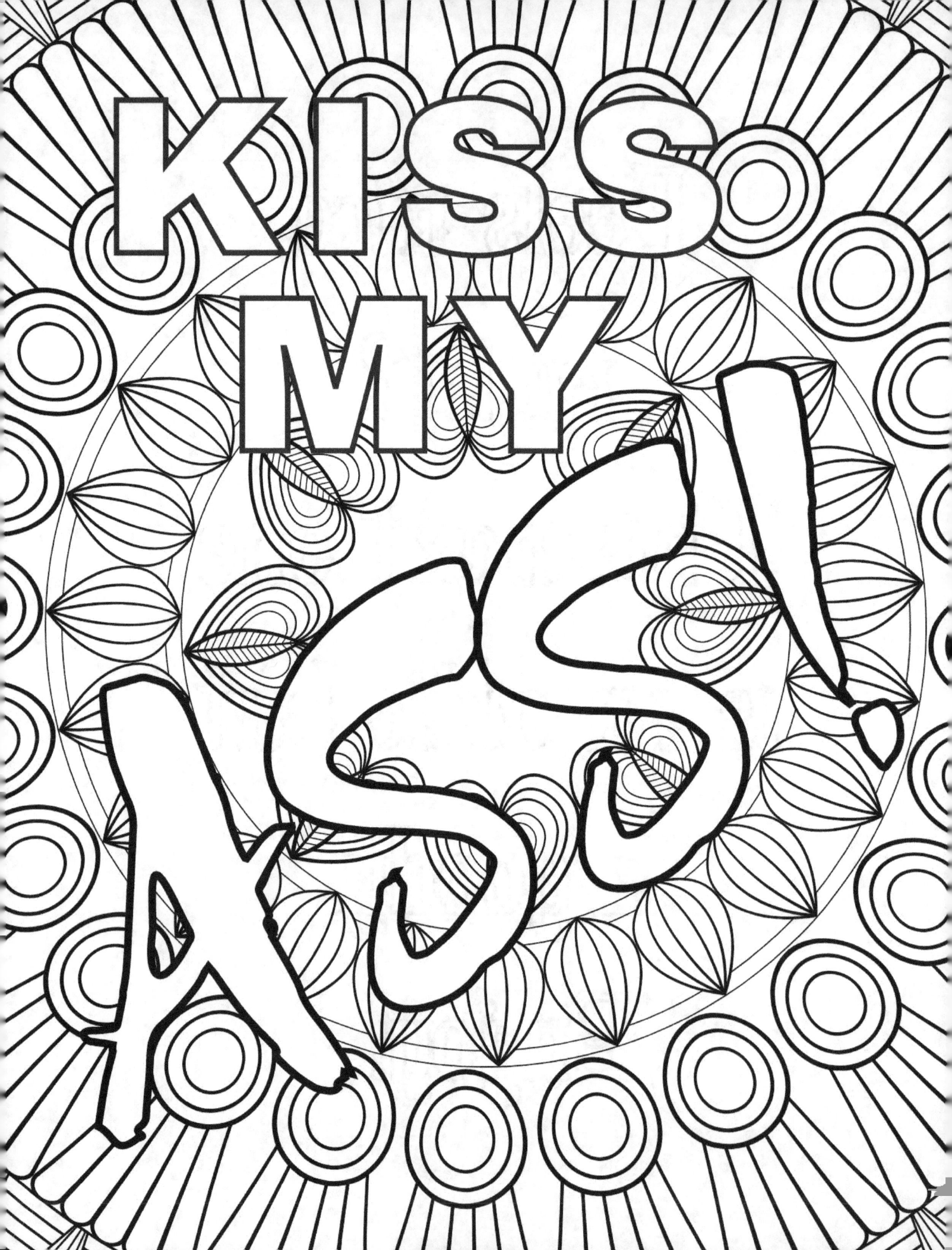

How does that
feel?
Only a little
better?
Alright, then
it's time to get
rude!

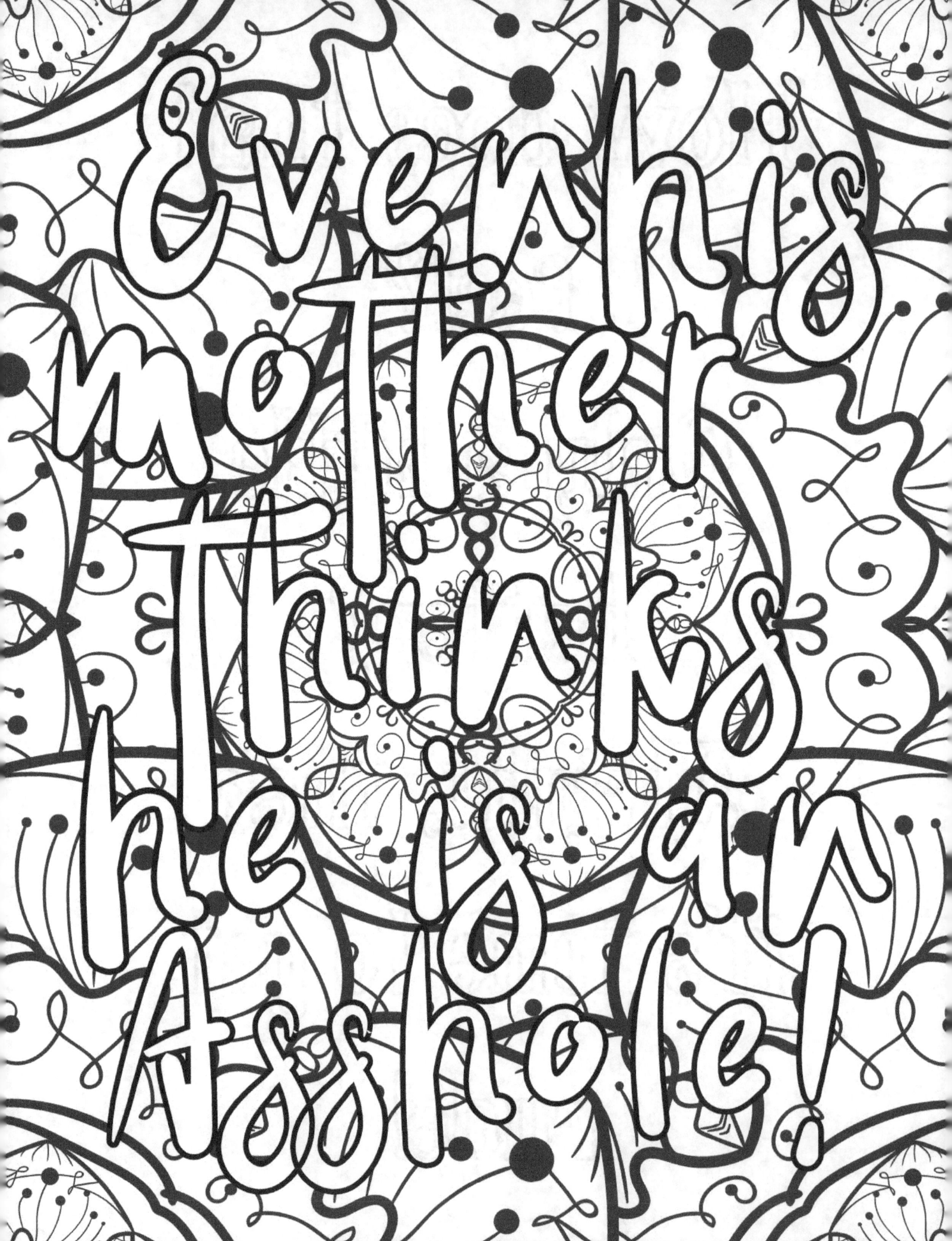

Oh yeah! Right up in their face with that one! Now let's make it personal!

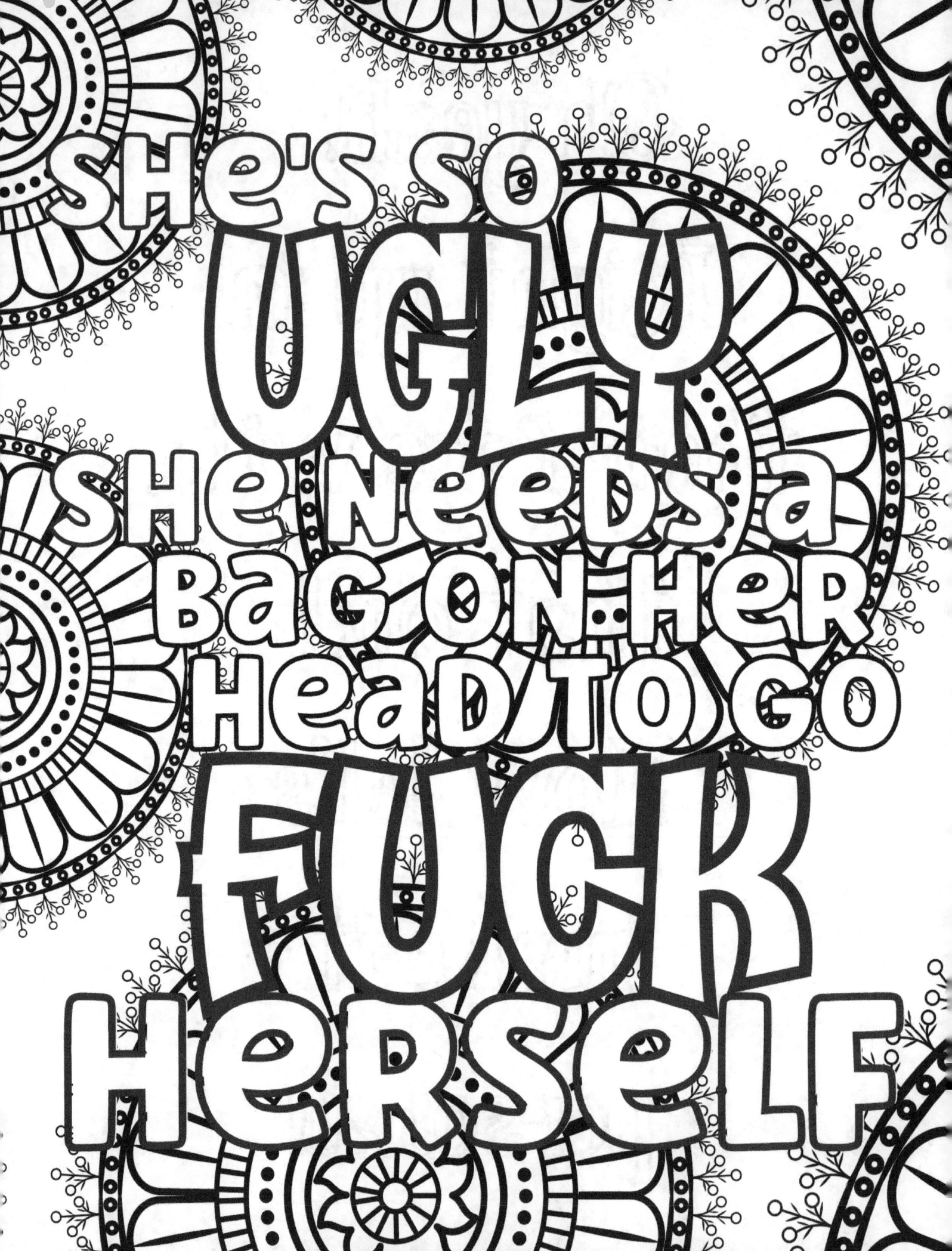

Ah, that's better. Feeling nice? All warmed up and ready to color a plain and simple truth?

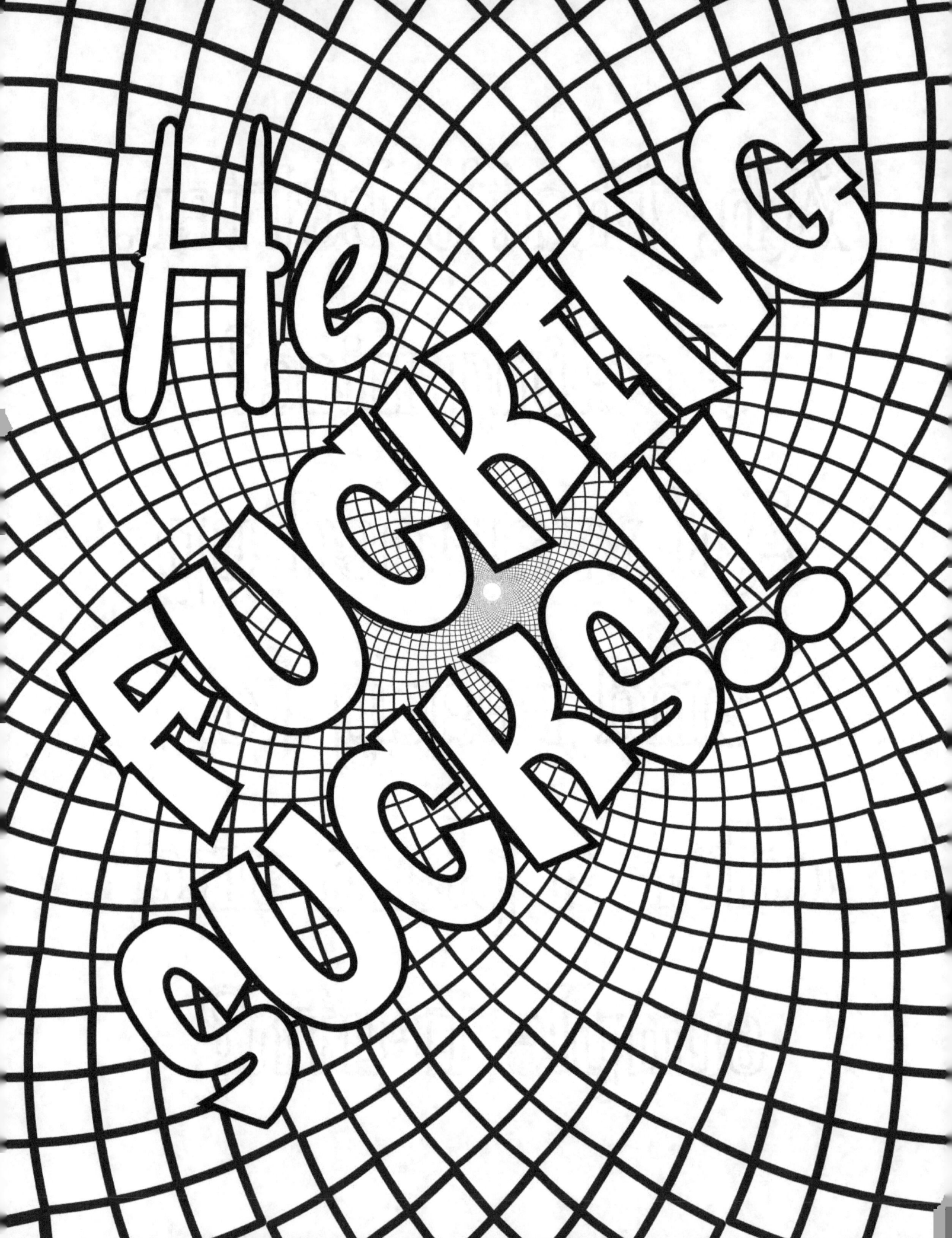

See, that's a little better right? Sometimes the simple truth is the best. Here's some more good old fashion truth.

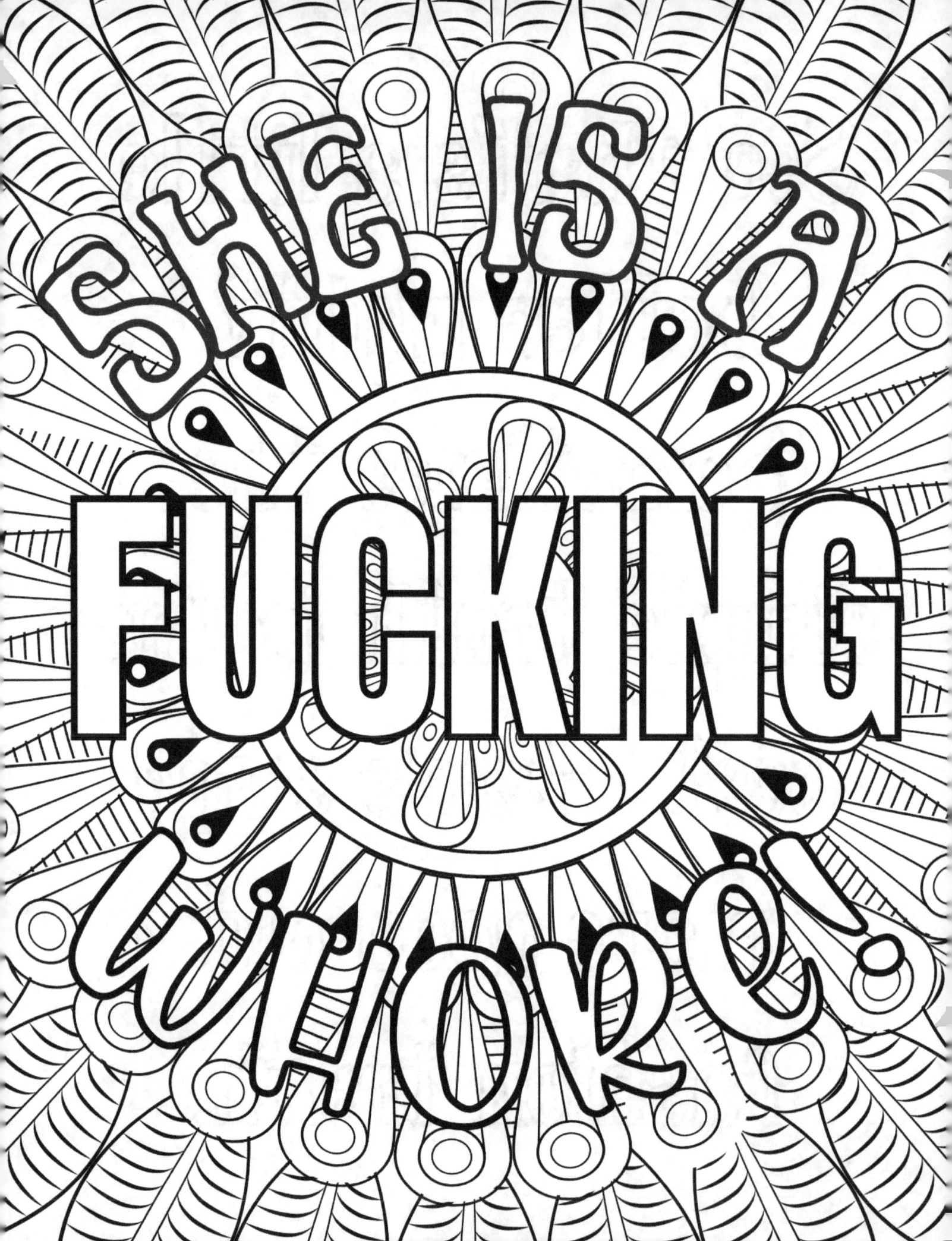

Well said.
Now, let's get
angry. In your
face, finger
pointing angry.
Let it out!

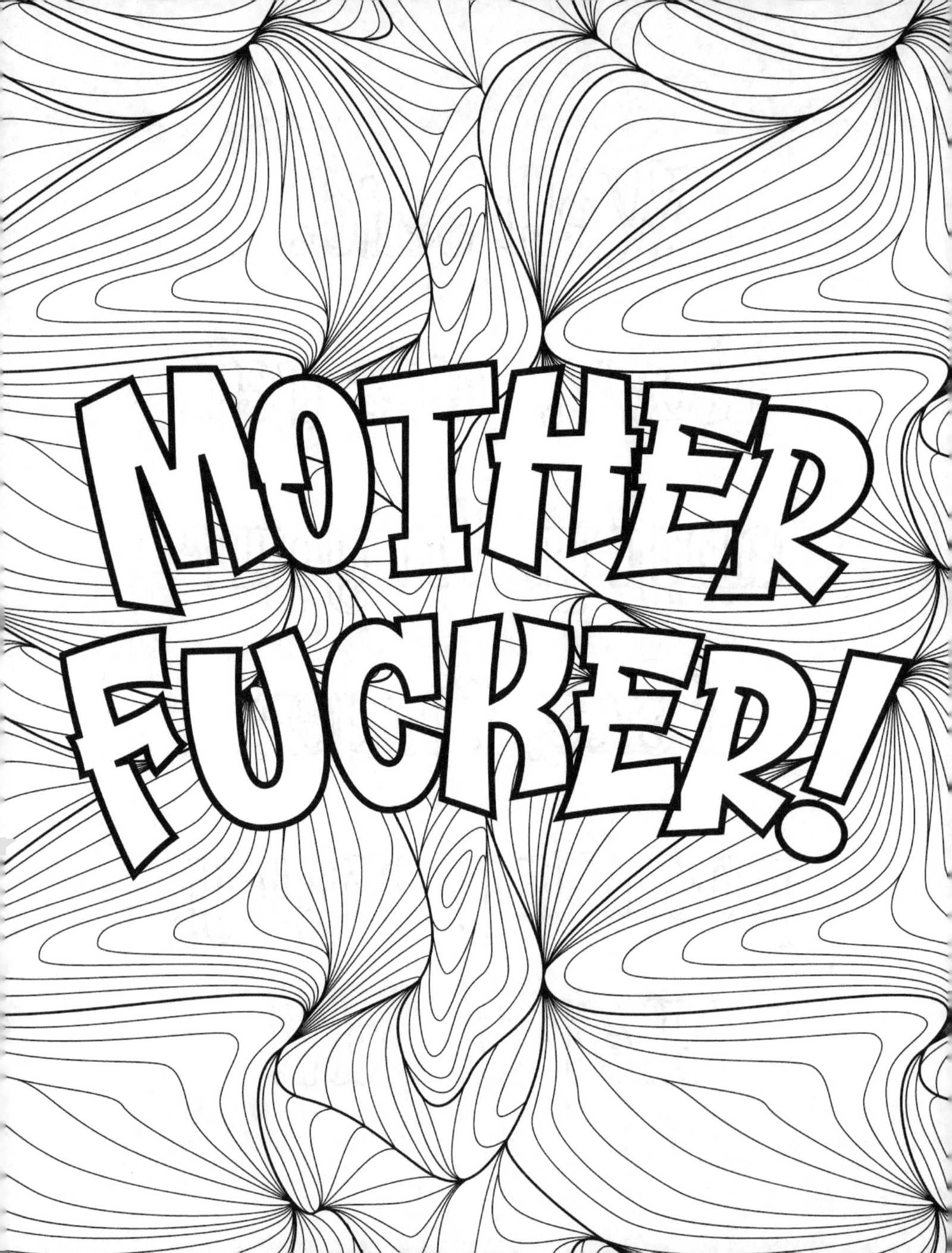

Sometimes, we just need to yell.
Now, let's get a little bit intellectual.

Sometimes it's best to just call them like you see them. And sometimes one swear word is just not enough...

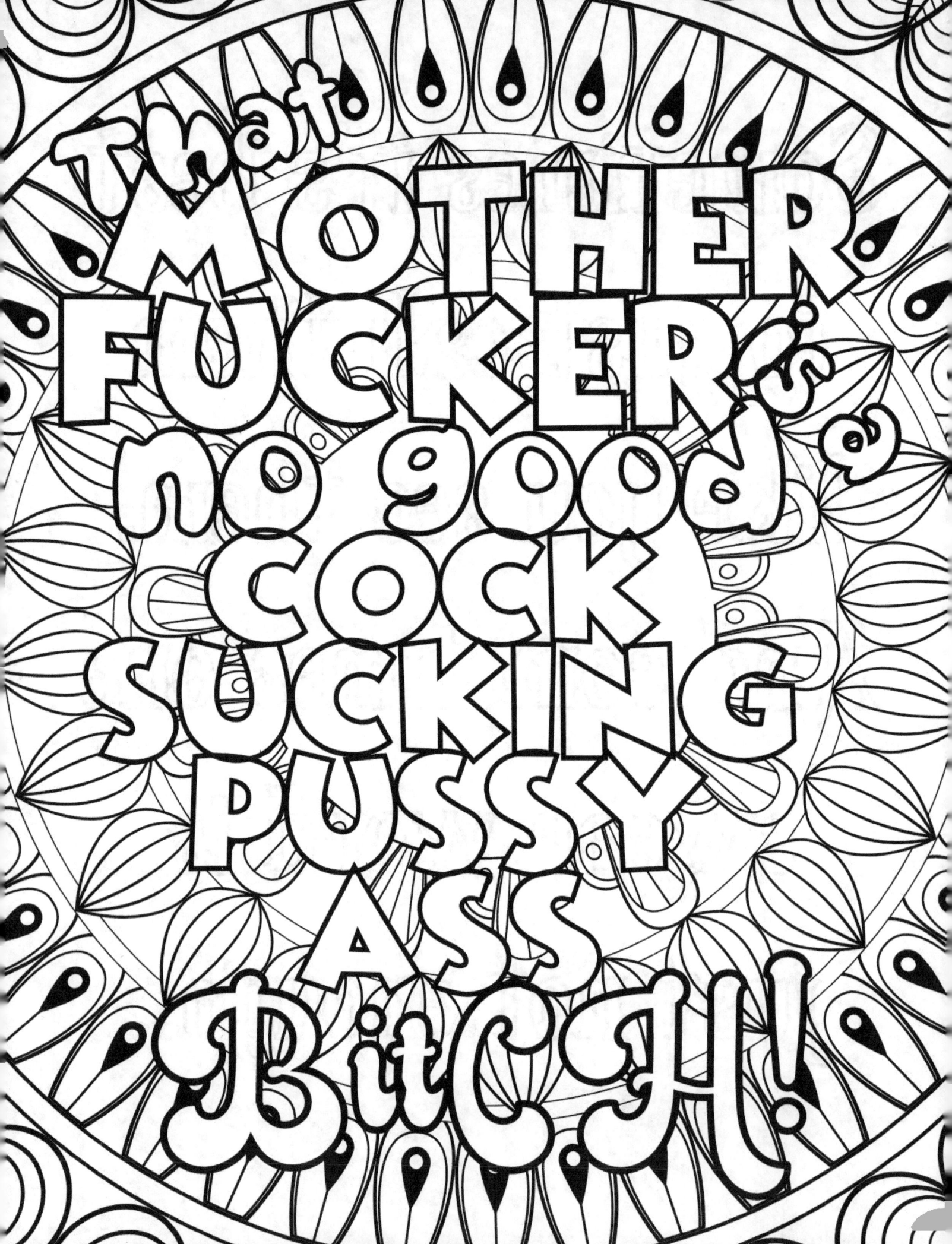

Aaahh! The pleasure of a proper bile filled rant...
Pure joy.
Now, let's get intellectual again.

HE IS A TRUE tight ass. THAT'S WHY nothing but SHIT comes out of HIS MOUTH!

Them be the facts, plain and simple. No bullshit here, unlike some people... Here's another fact for you!

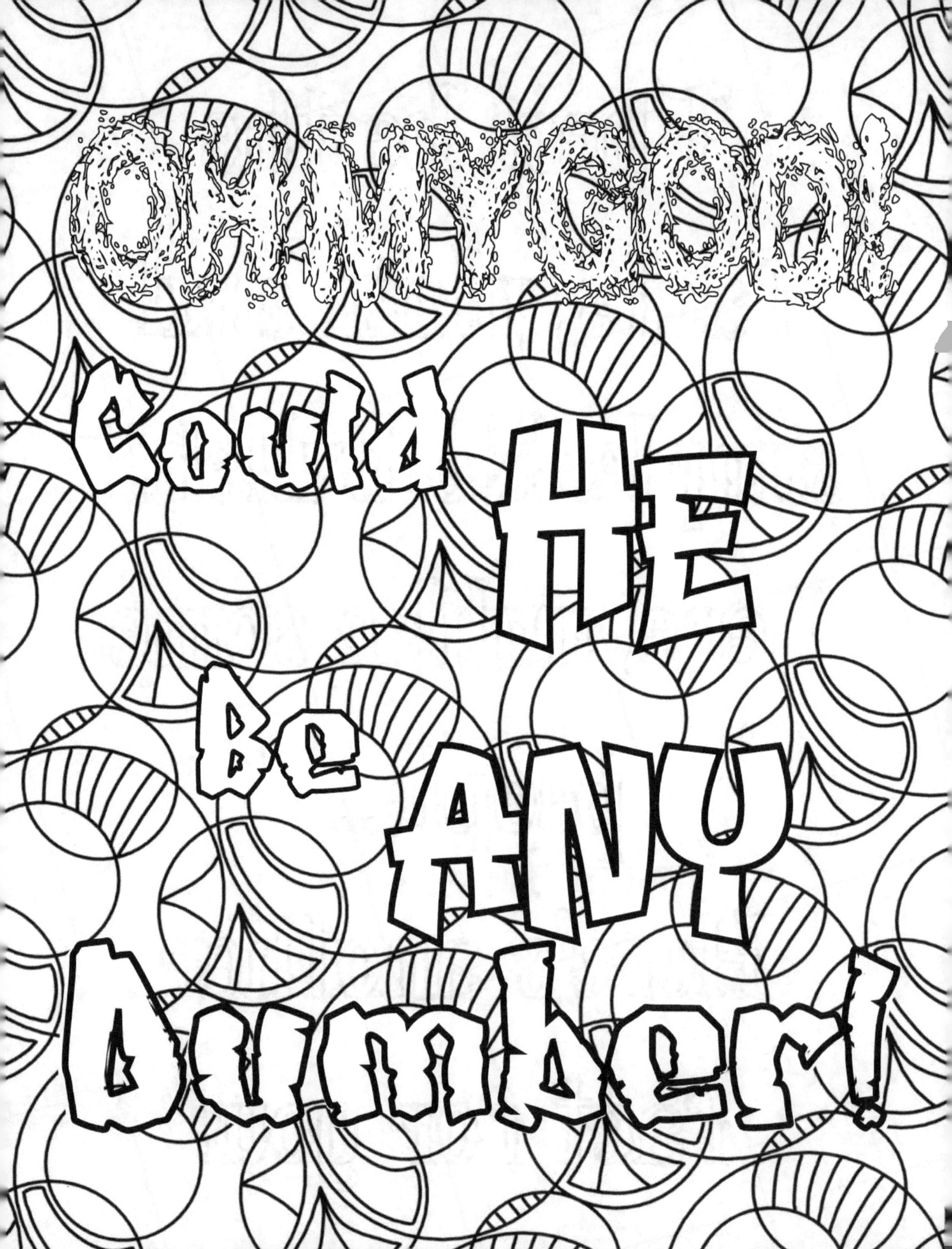

We all have to work with 1 or 2 of those! (Or we marry one...) Alright, let's get political!

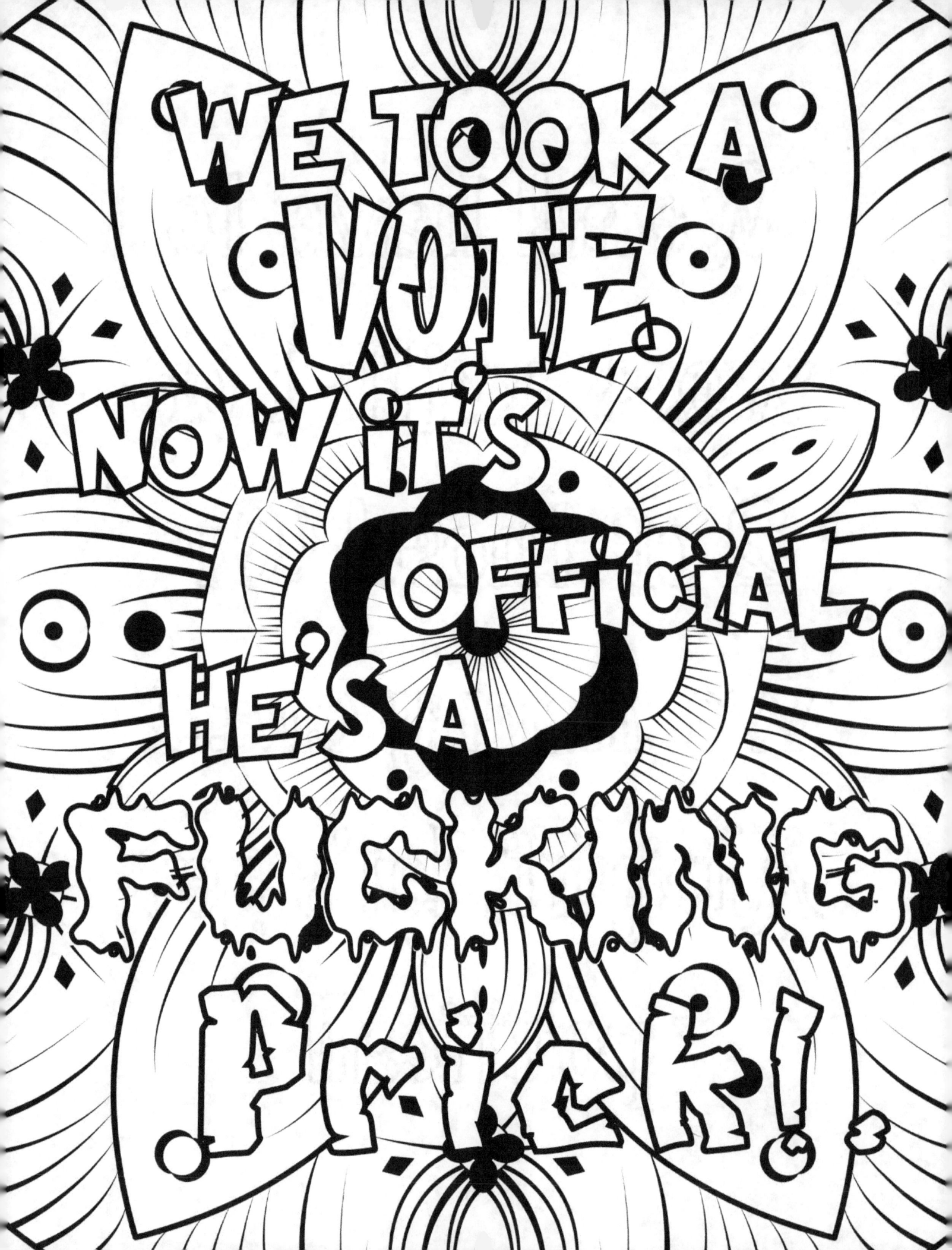

Ahh the power of democracy! God bless the right to vote!

Let's move on to how they make you feel...

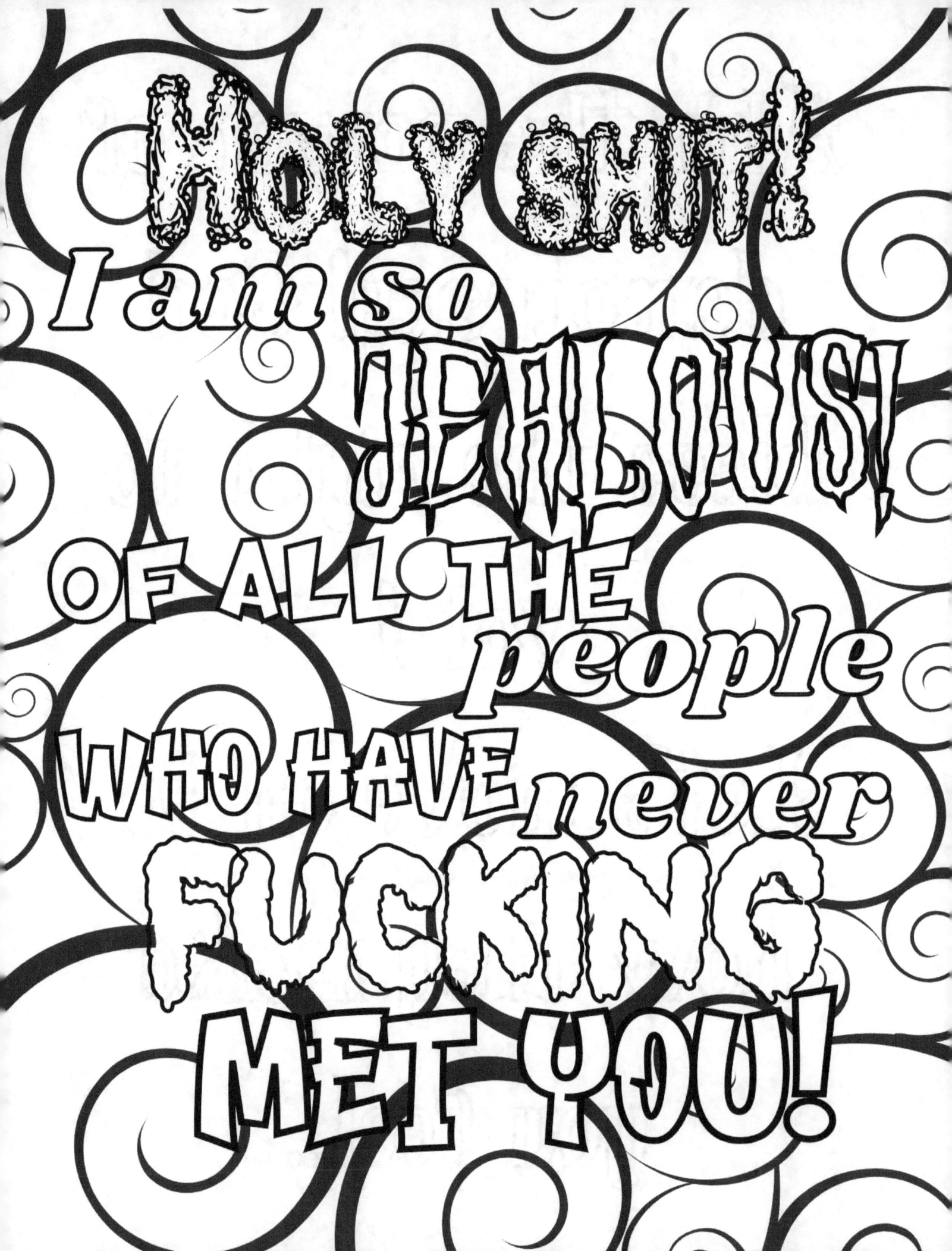

Normally, I'd say jealousy is a bad thing... Not today! Next, let's give some detailed instructions.

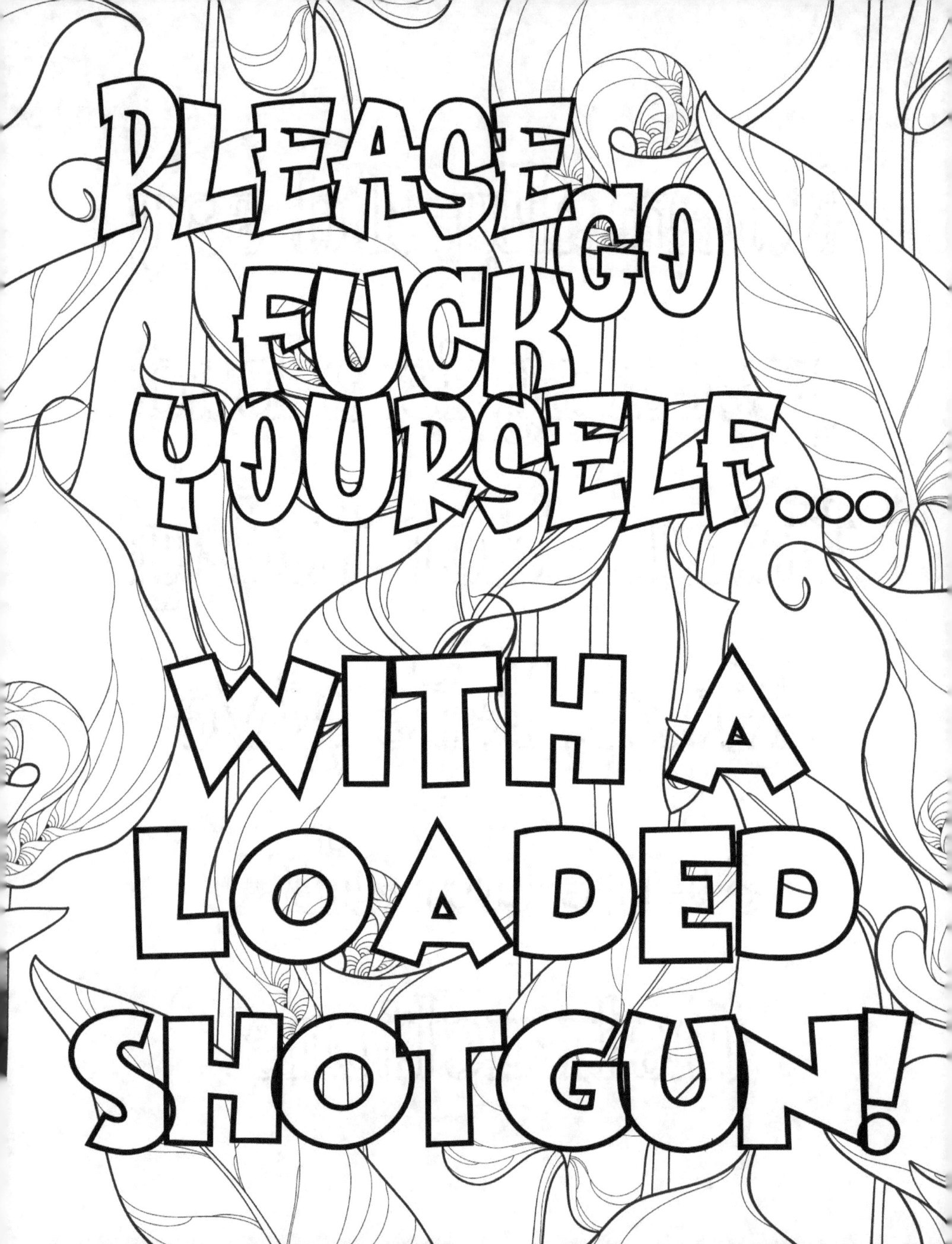

Yep, some people need a proper plan of action! OK, for some people you have to combine insults.

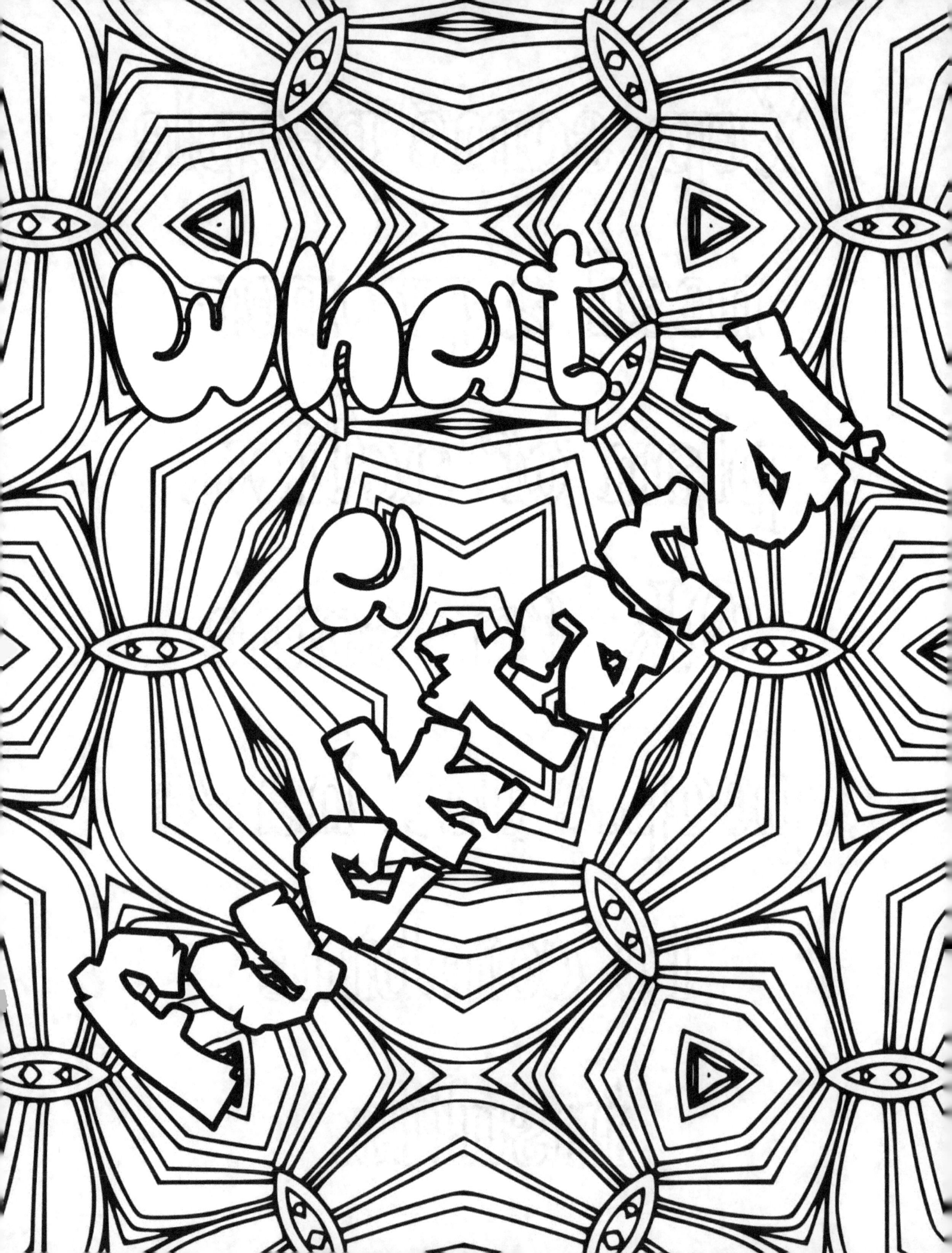

Feel better, now?
Nothing like
coloring in a good
scream.
Time to get nasty
again!

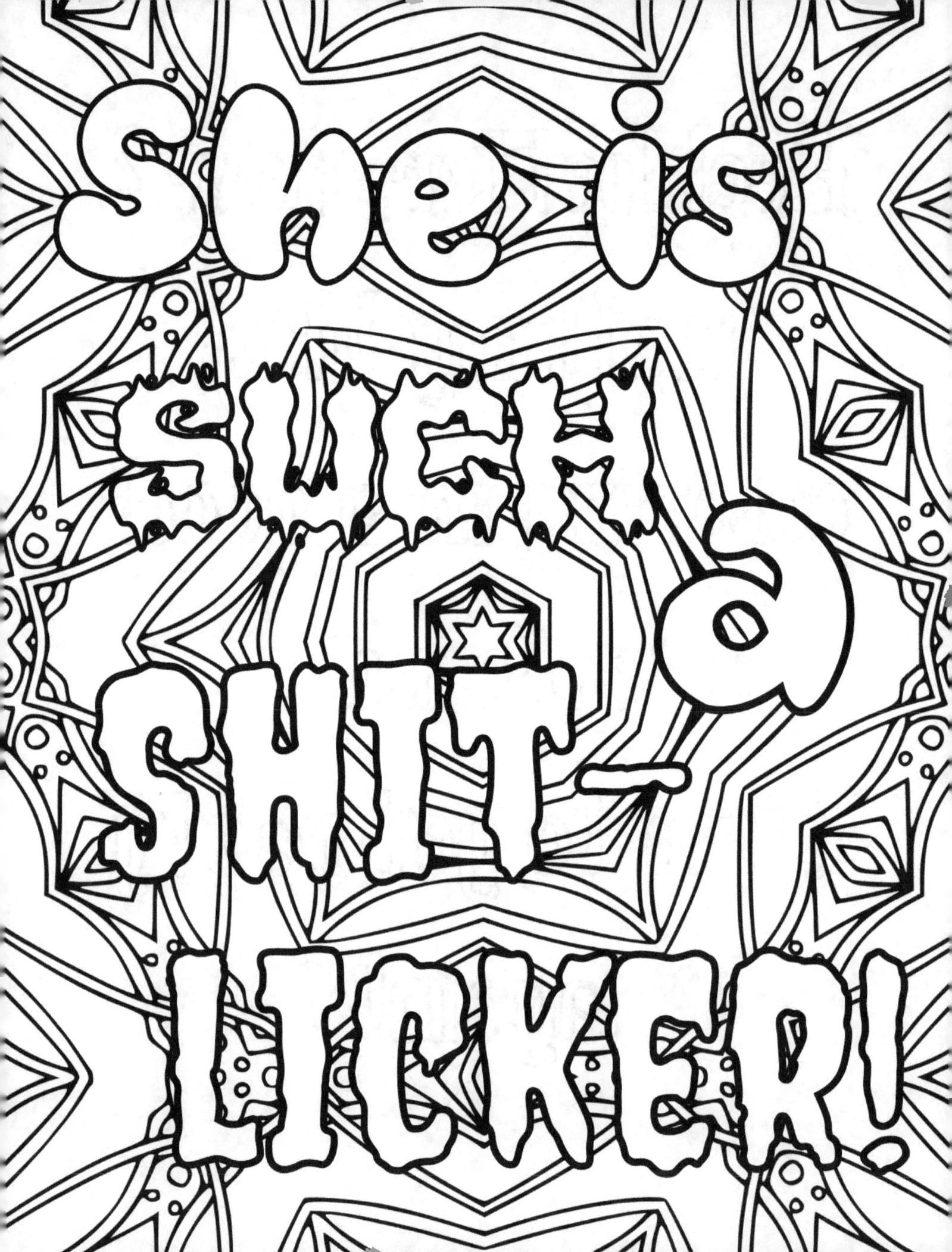

Some bitches are just low. And some bitches are in need of a sewing kit!

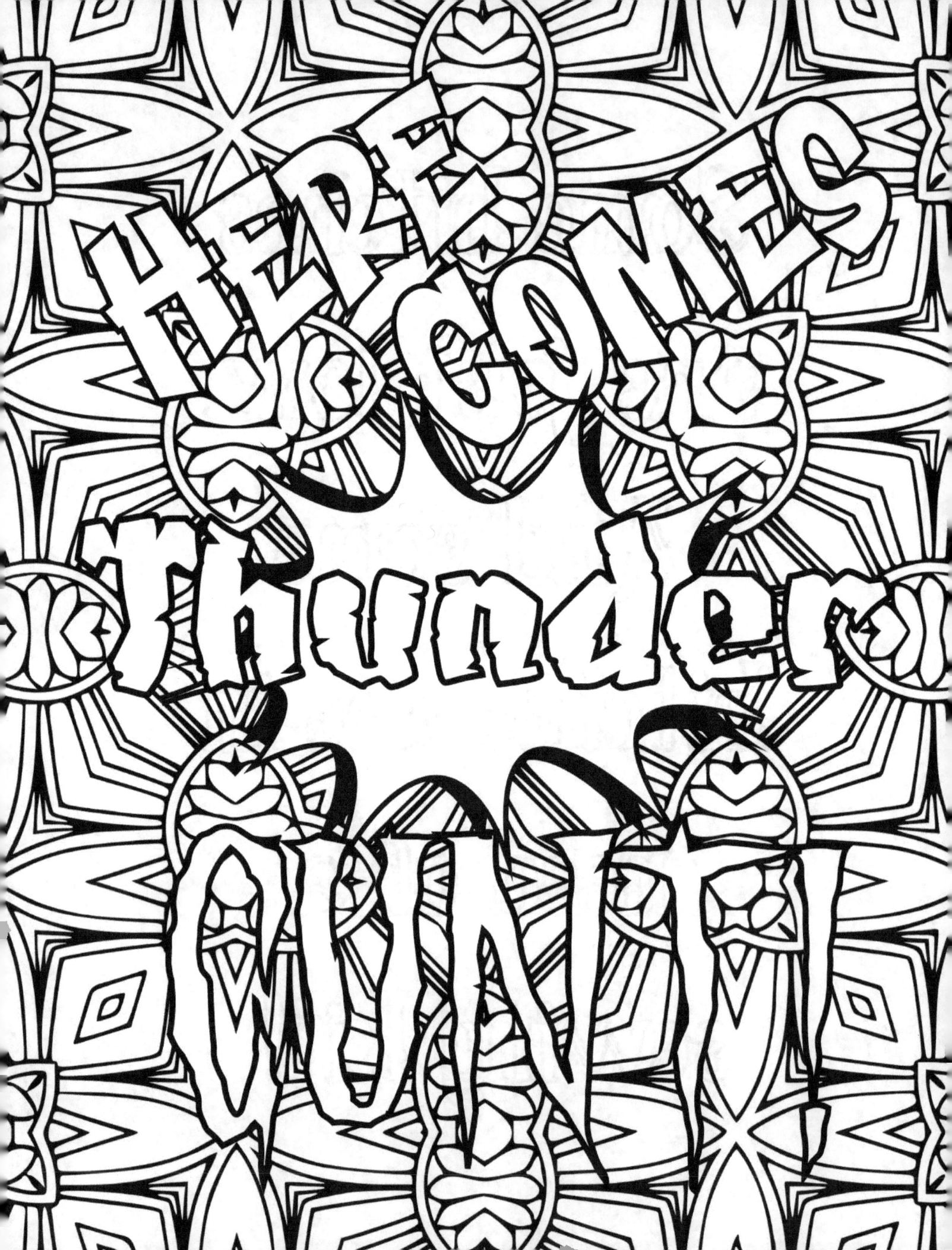

Loud and Nasty! You just don't need people like that in your life, ya know? And some are even worse.

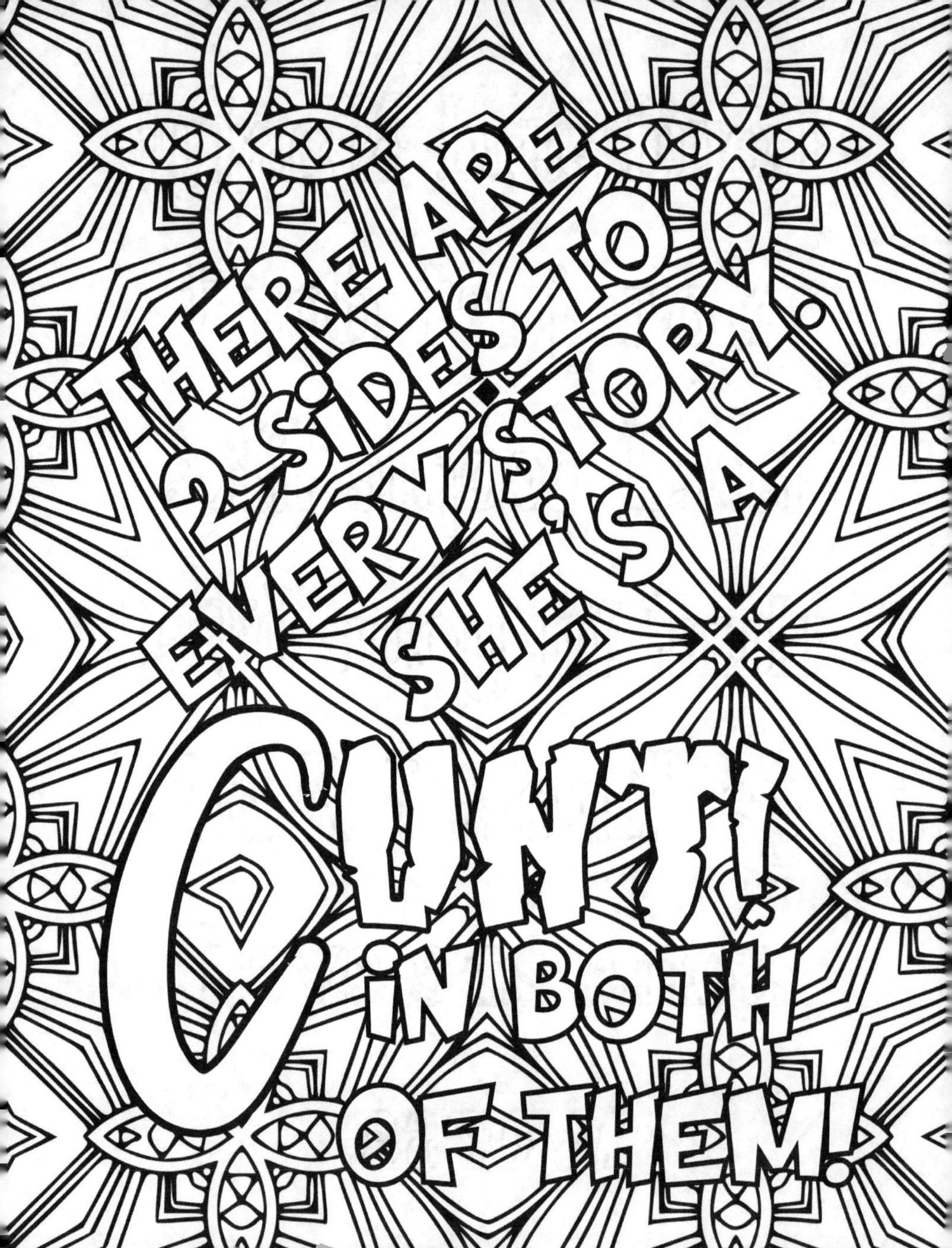

They don't deserve you! Walk away. 'nuff said. Let's look at the male problem once again.

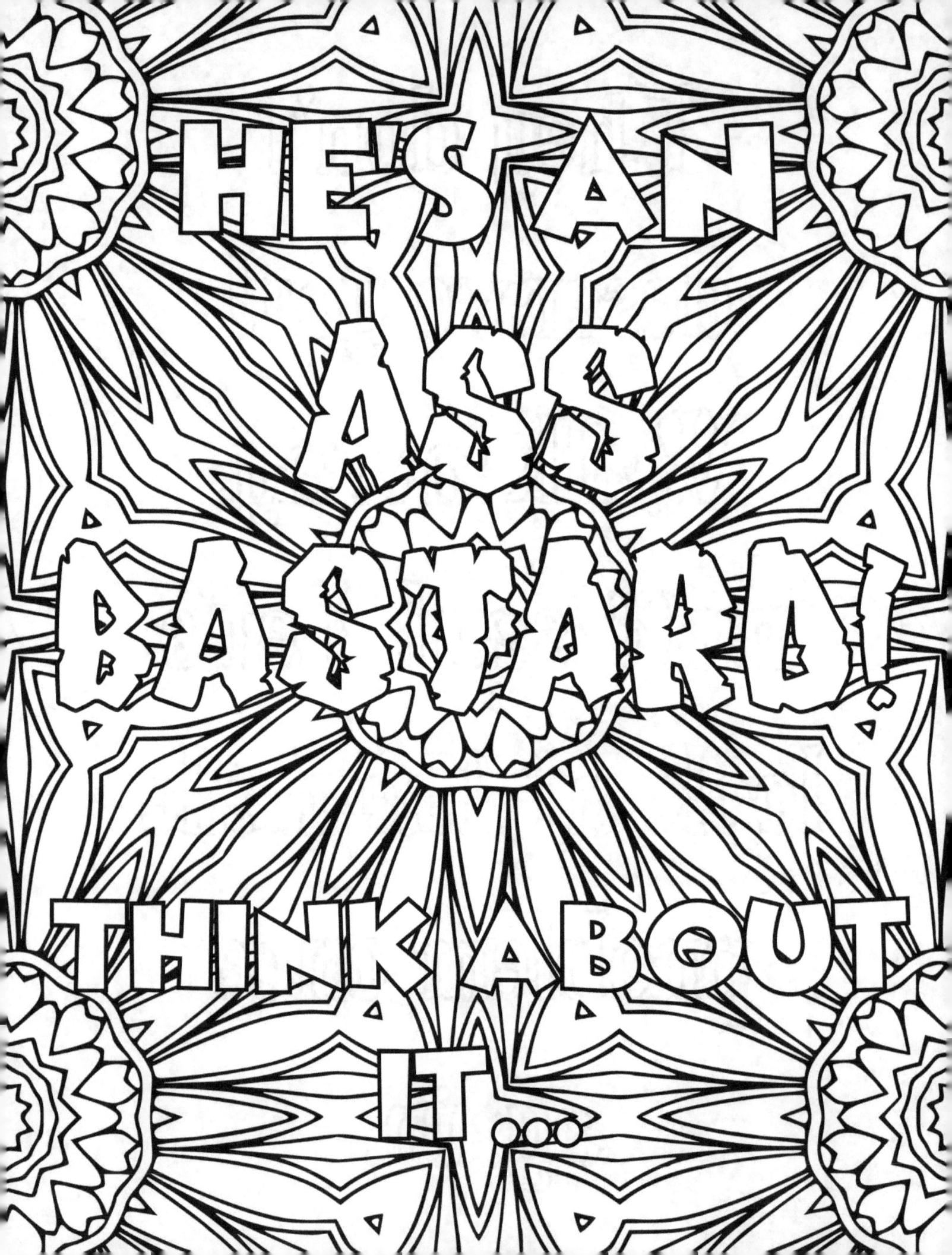

They ain't worth
a second of your
time...
Now let's get
into some
philosophy.

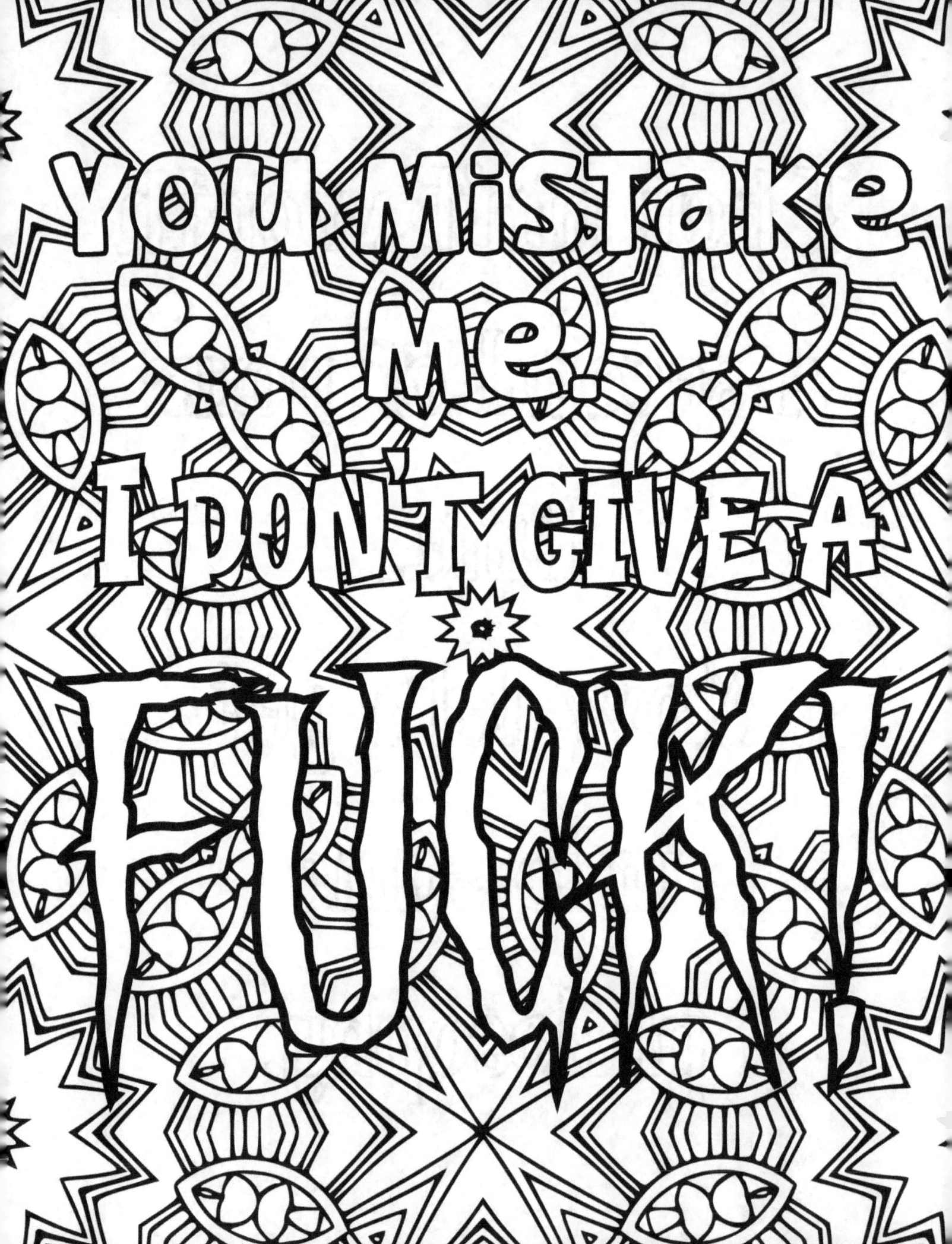

Ahh, yes! There is true power in not caring.

It's vital when you run into one of these useless bastards...

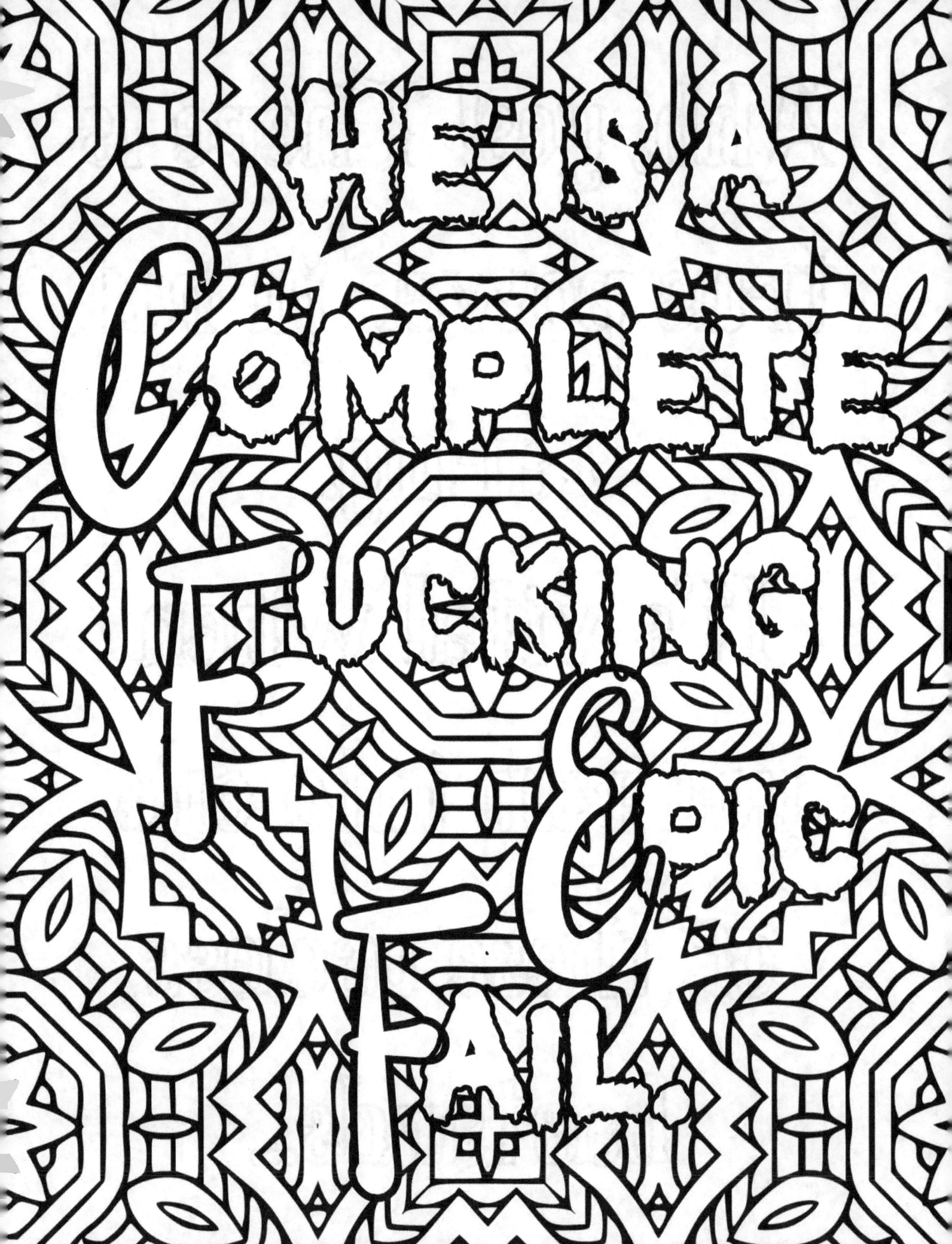

You'd feel sorry for them if they weren't such giant dicks...Then there's these low-life slime-balls!

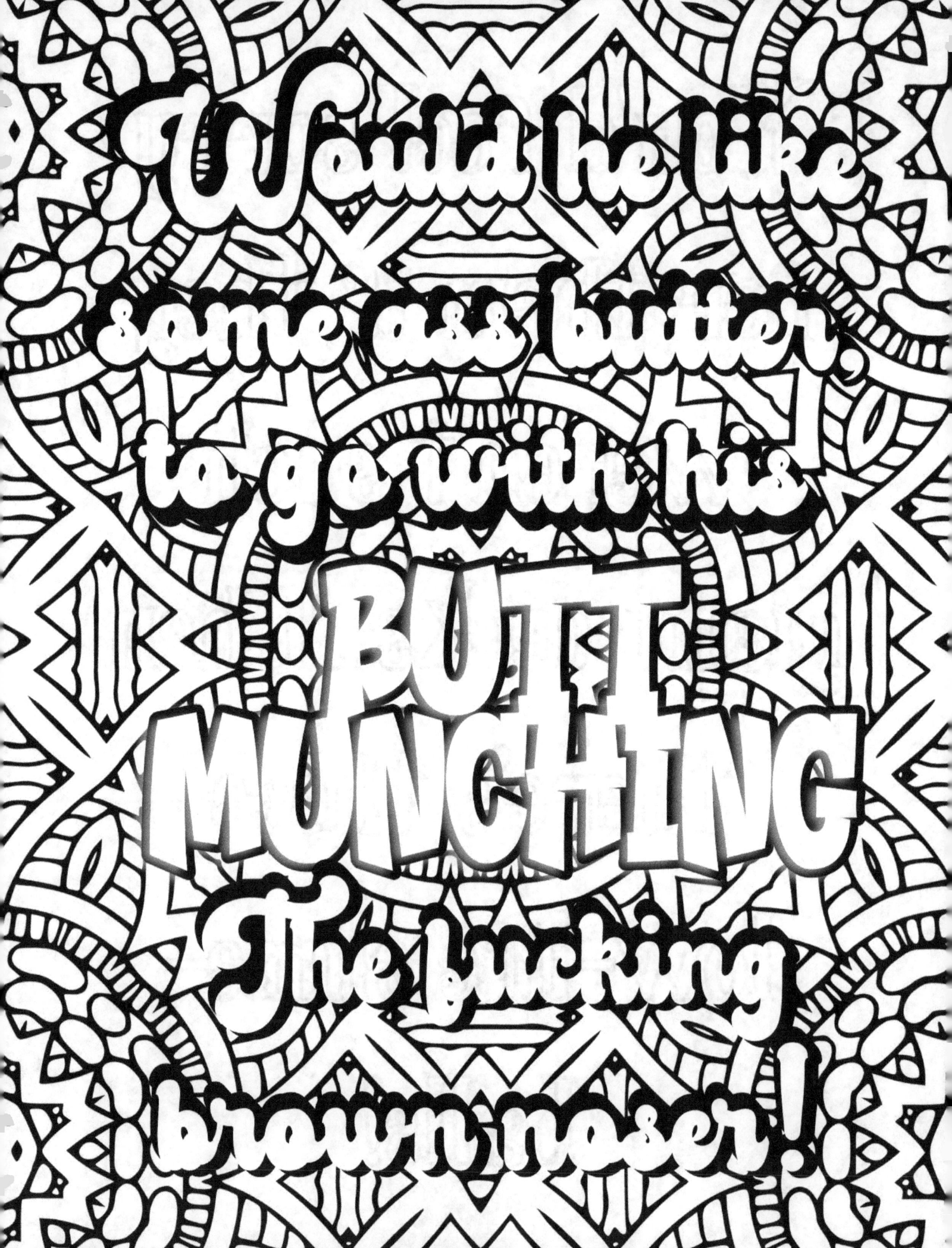

Hard to even be in the same room with those fuckers! Then there's the stress-about-nothing twats!

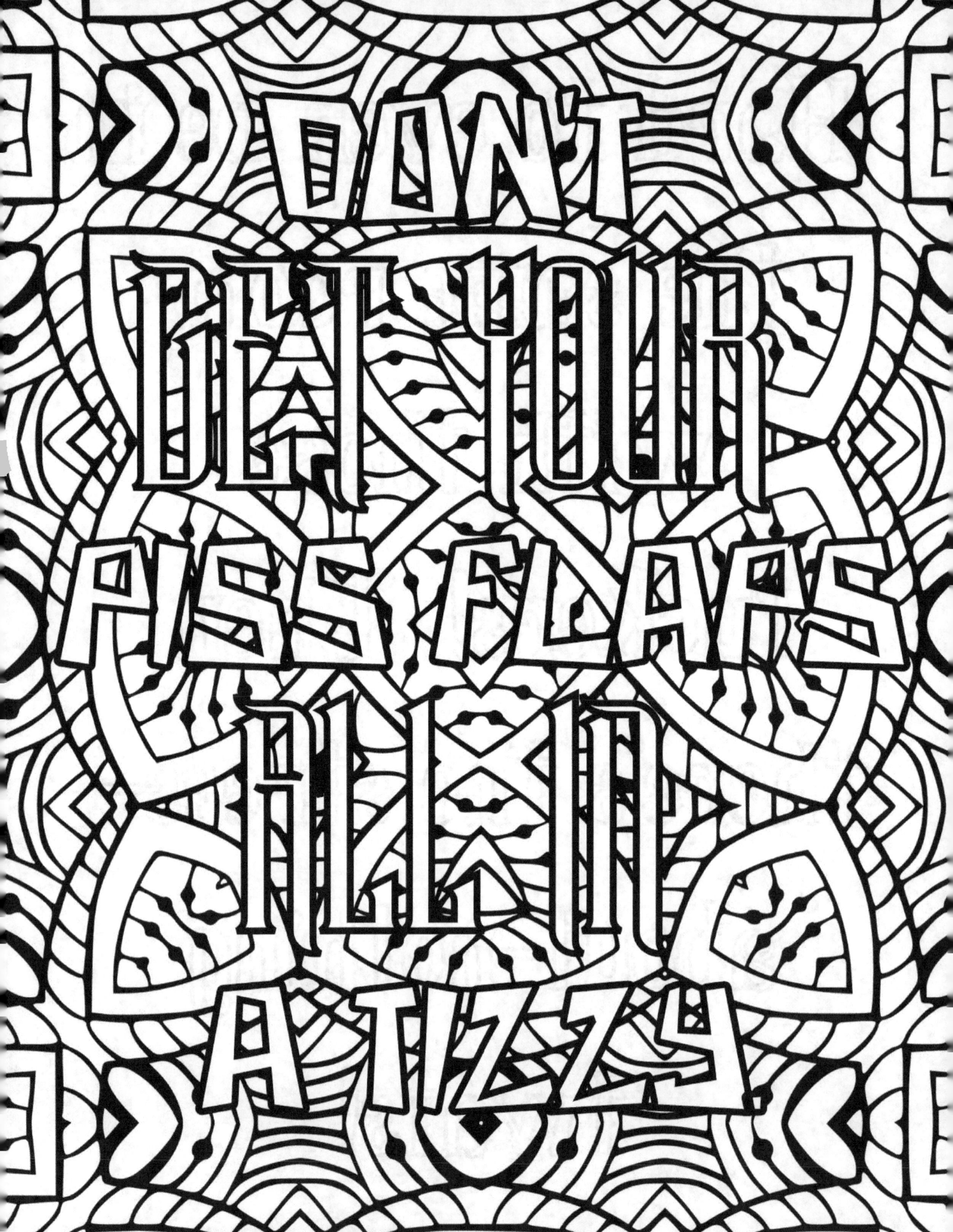

They need to take a deep breath, somewhere far away... Then there's those who think every dick is theirs!

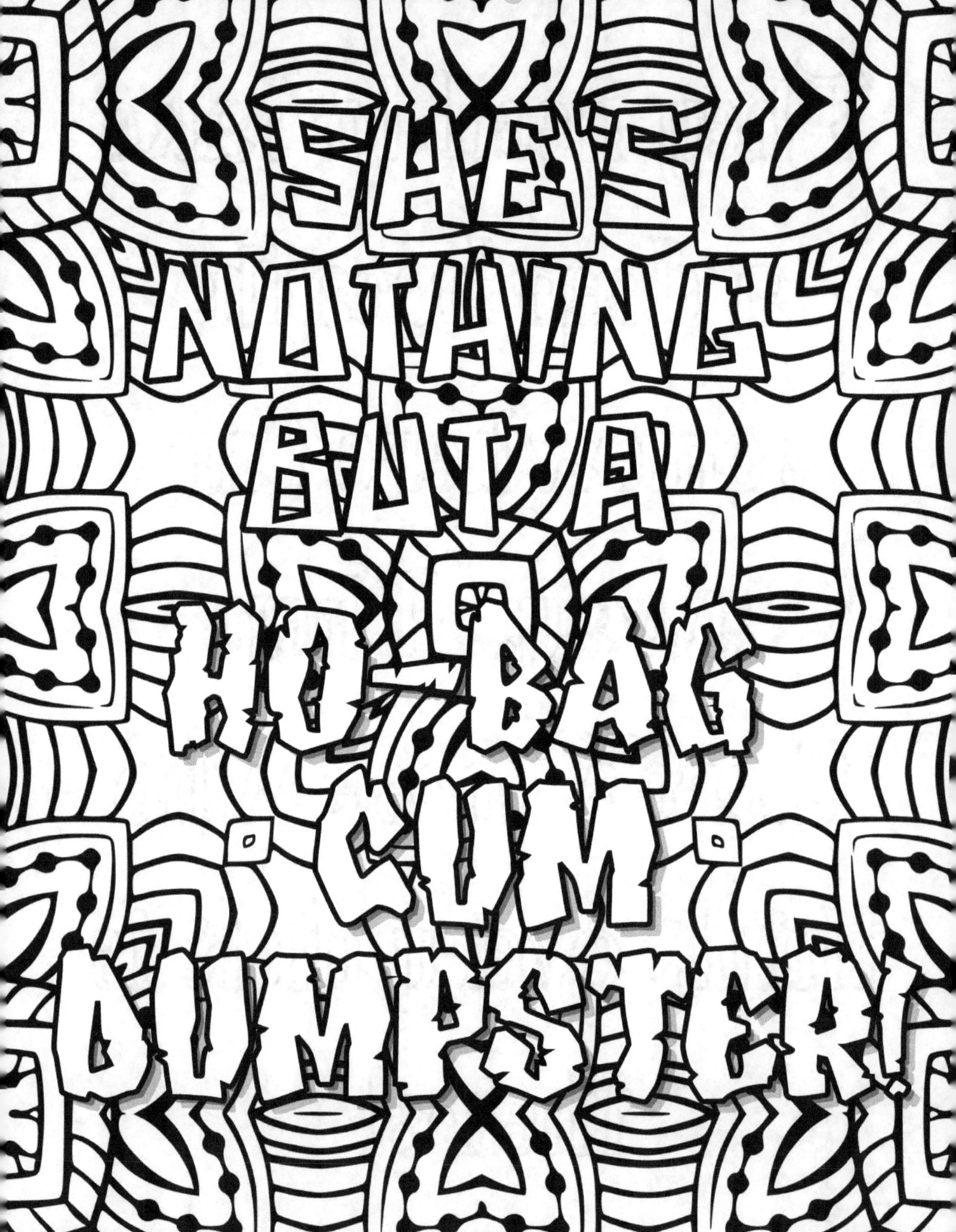

Disgusting creatures who deserve their STD's!

Let's move onto the physically impaired!

At the end of the day, they're just useless... Sad really... Not! Next we have the politicians disease...

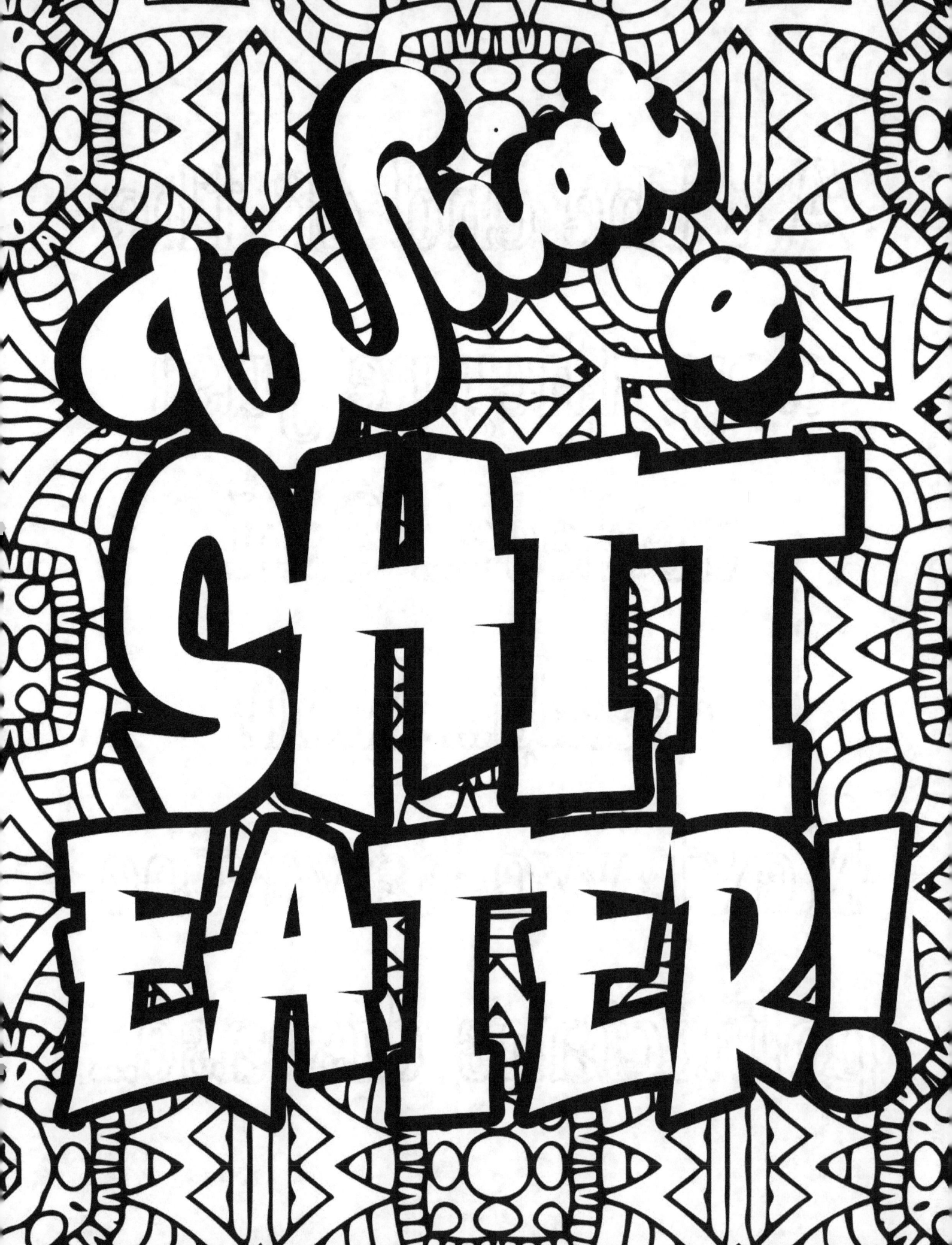

Fucker's will do anything to get ahead! Well if that's true, then this next one is a suggestion just for them!

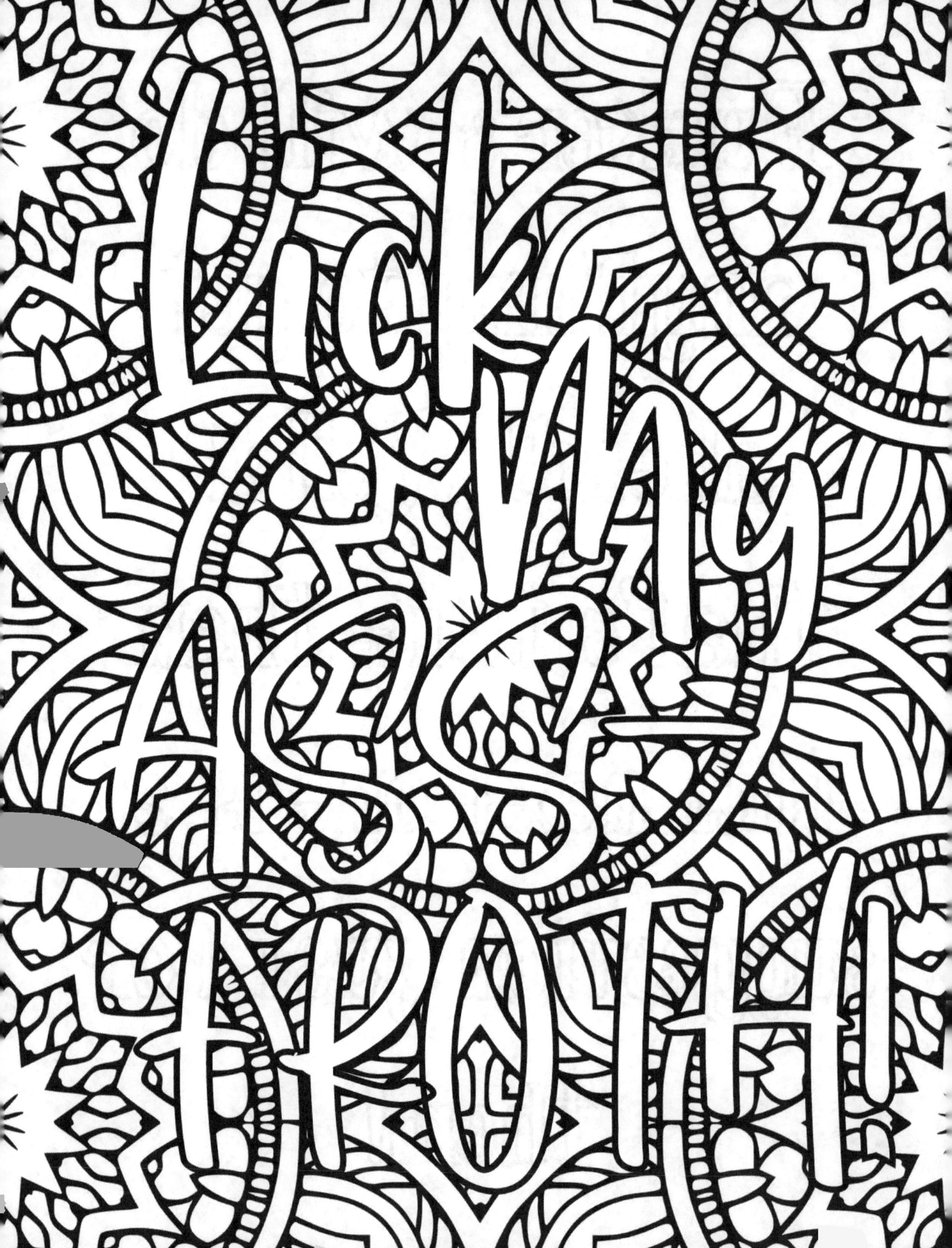

The sad thing is, those nasty fuckers would probably do it! Then there's these vile fucks!

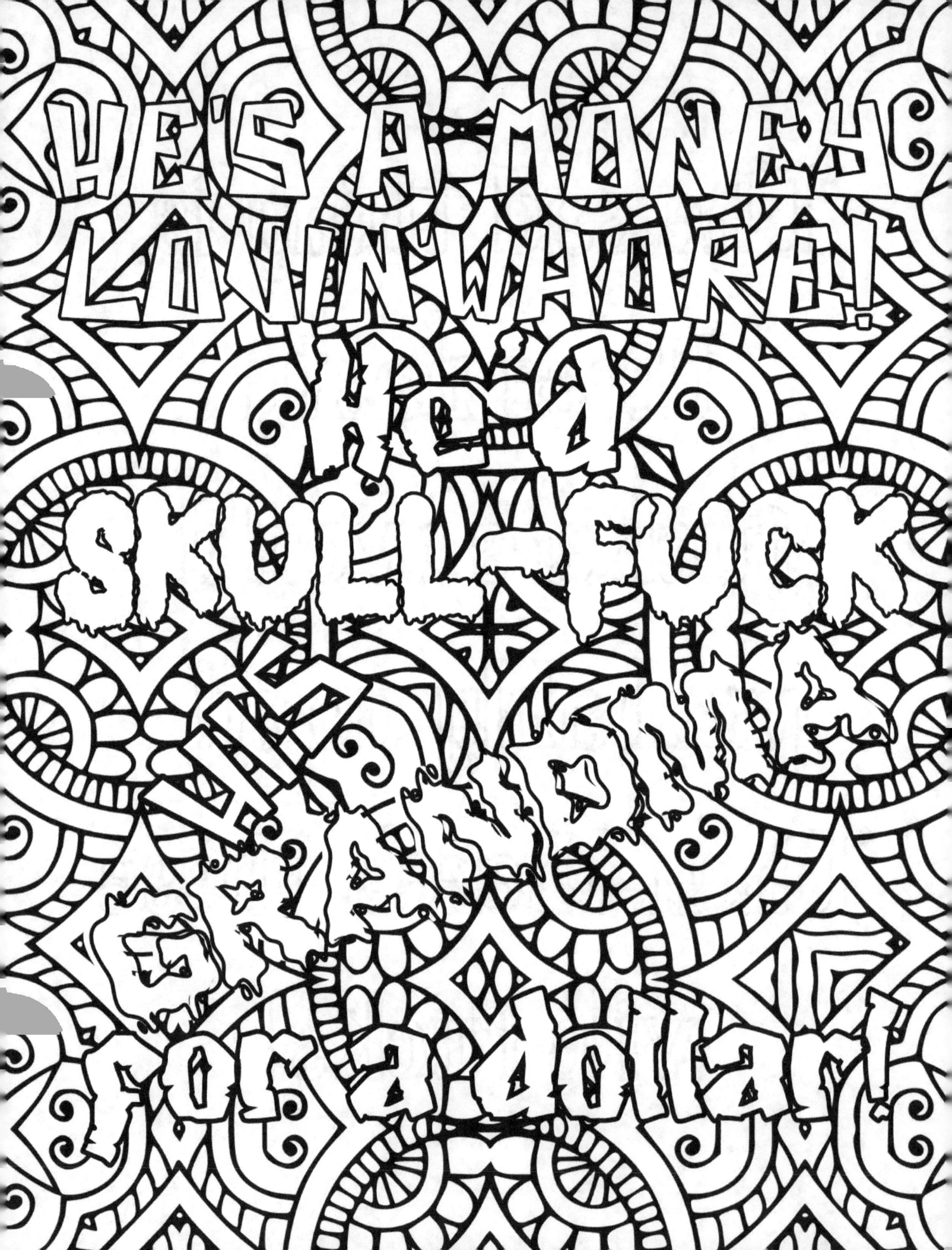

The root of all evil... 'nuff said. Moving on, some people just don't understand simple hygiene.

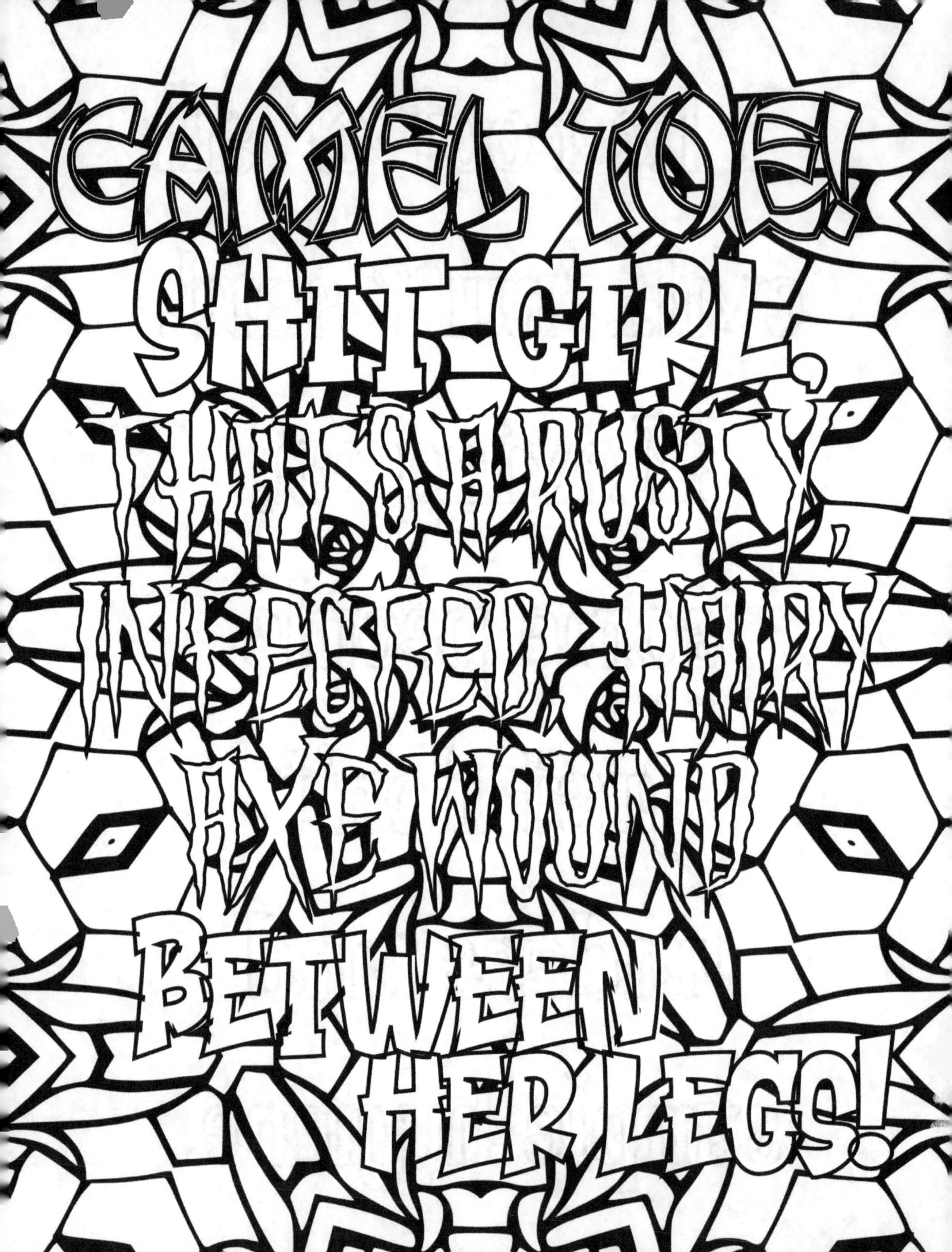

Clean your shit up! That's all I'm saying.

Now some people need their own special category.

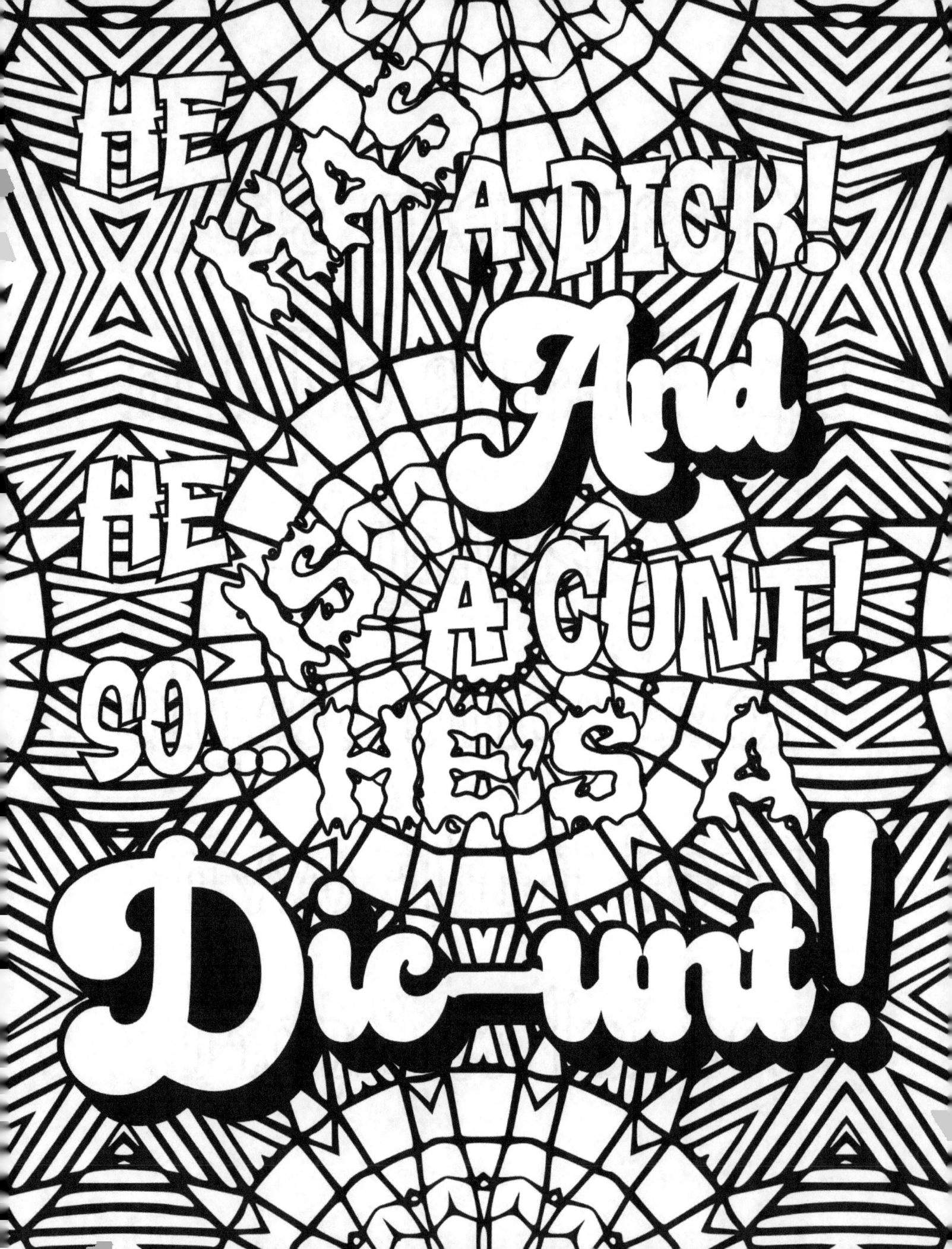

The worst of both worlds... Feels like it's time for a good screaming rant!

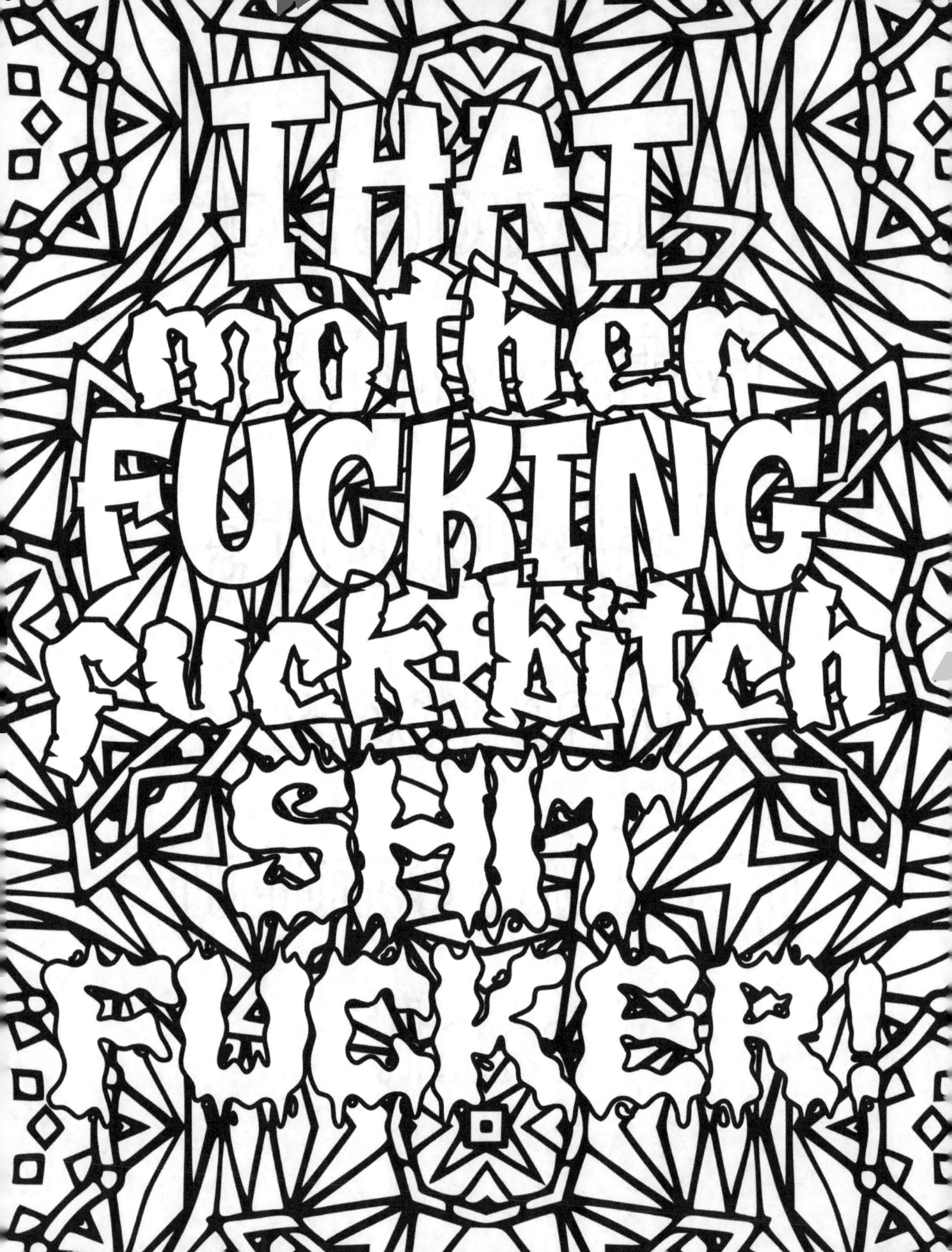

Oh yeah! That feels goooood! Time to tell some ugly, personal truth!

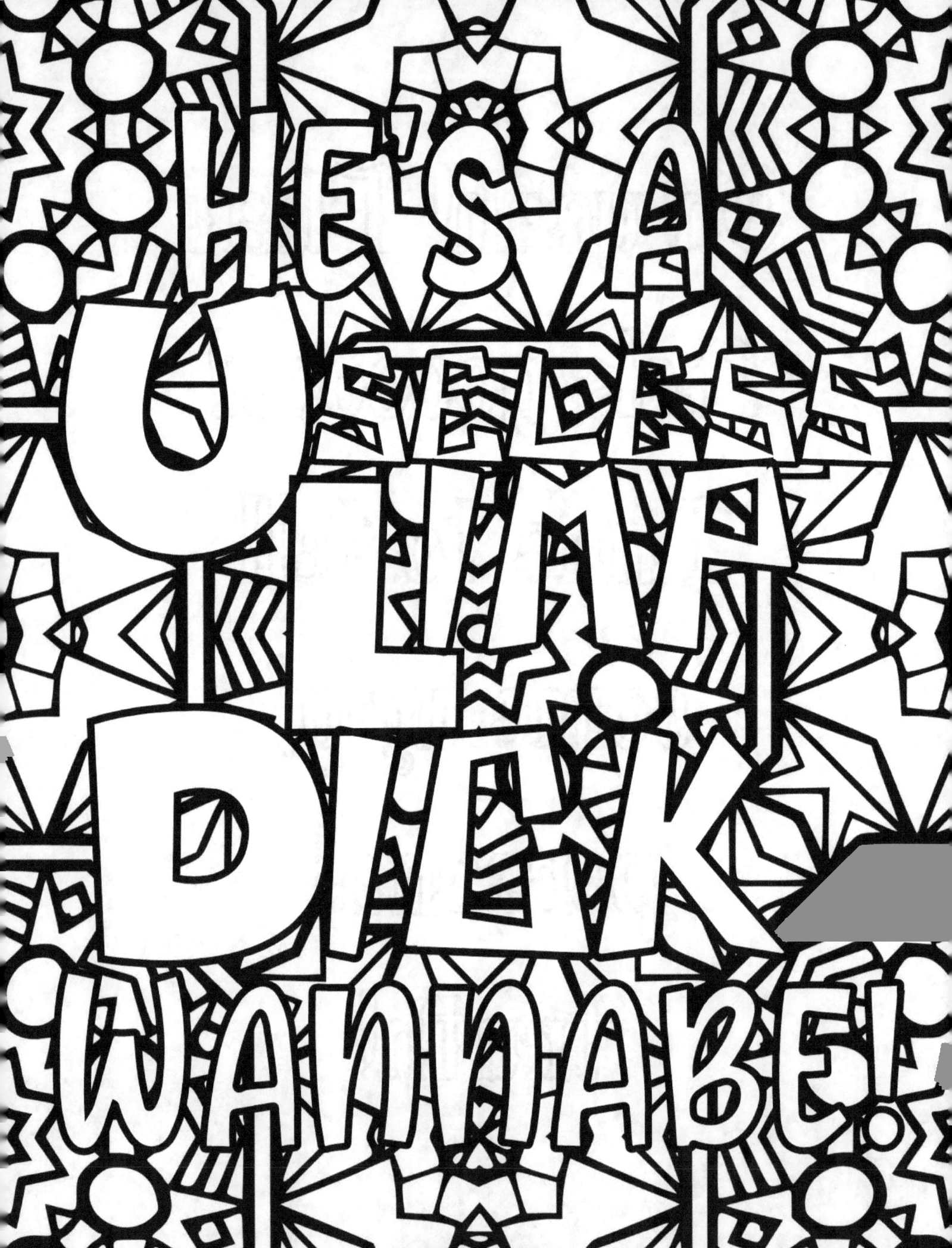

A pathetic embarrassment to the entire race...

Alright! Let's get angry again!

Ahh, the complete dismissal of a useless human being, so satisfying... Onto social media sluts!

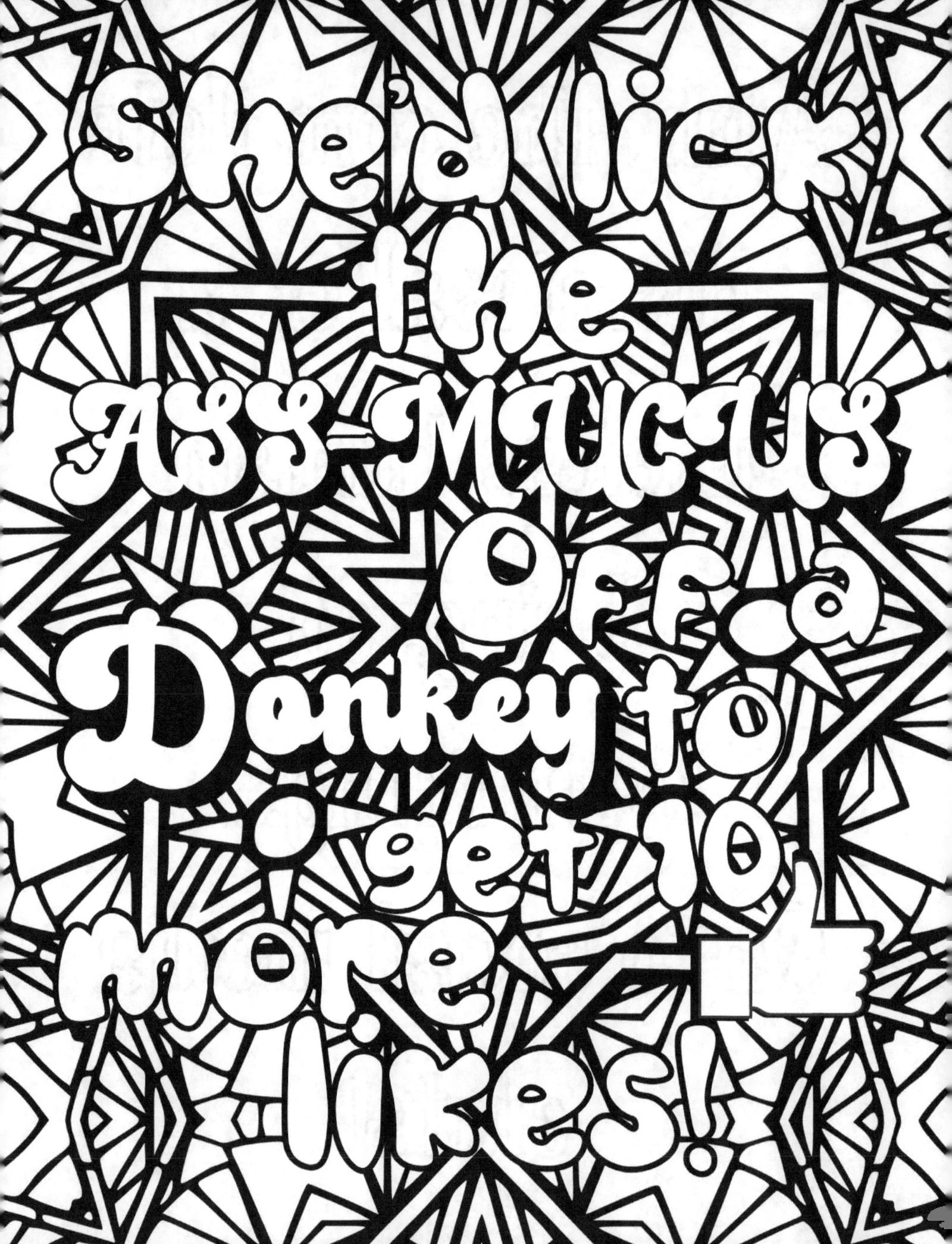

Now that's nasty!
Your phone ain't
your friend
ass-hat!
Now a personal
favorite.

She gets everyone from time to time, but some people... Onto another kind of annoying shit for brains...

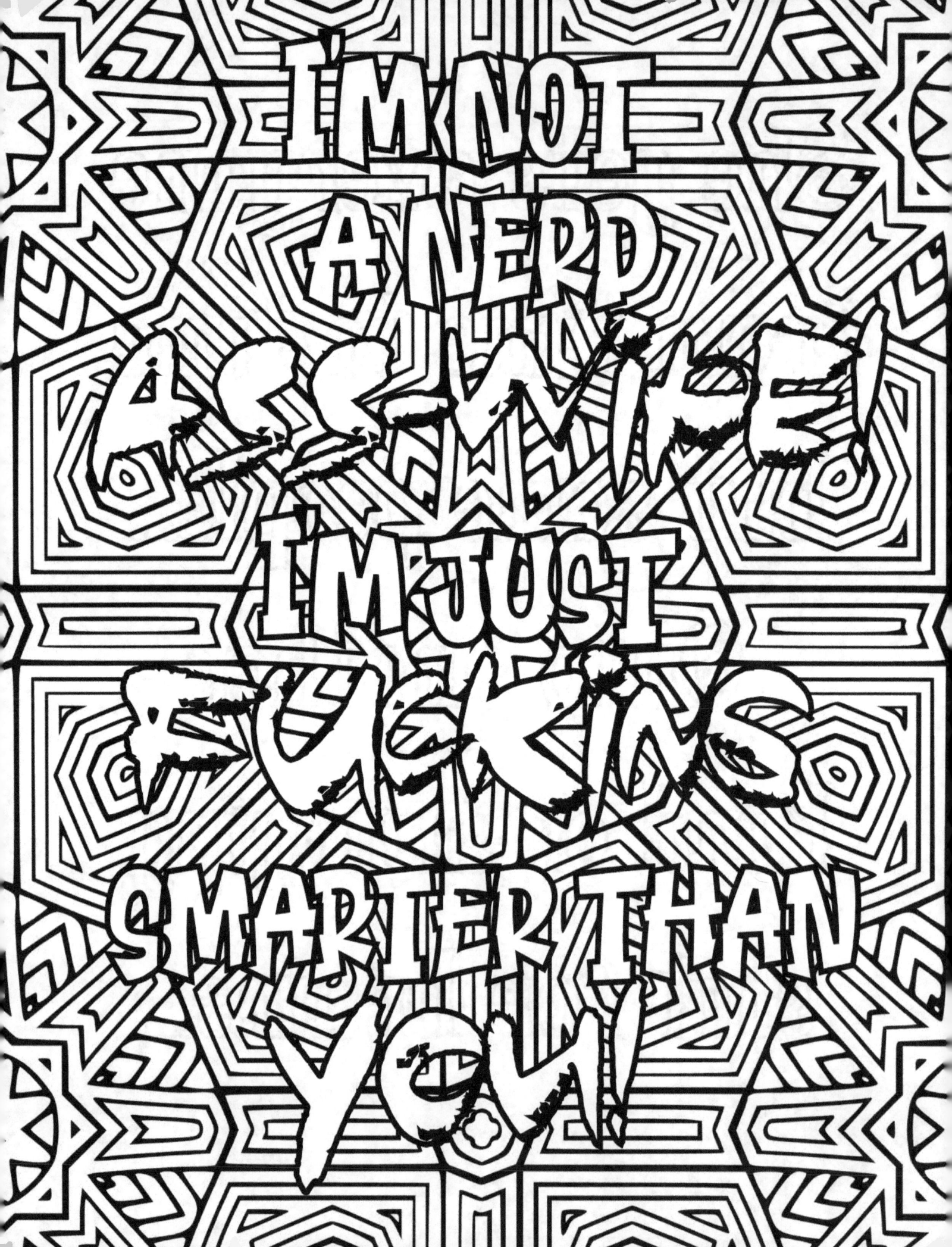

You've gotta speak slowly around some people.
Then there's those who shouldn't speak at all...

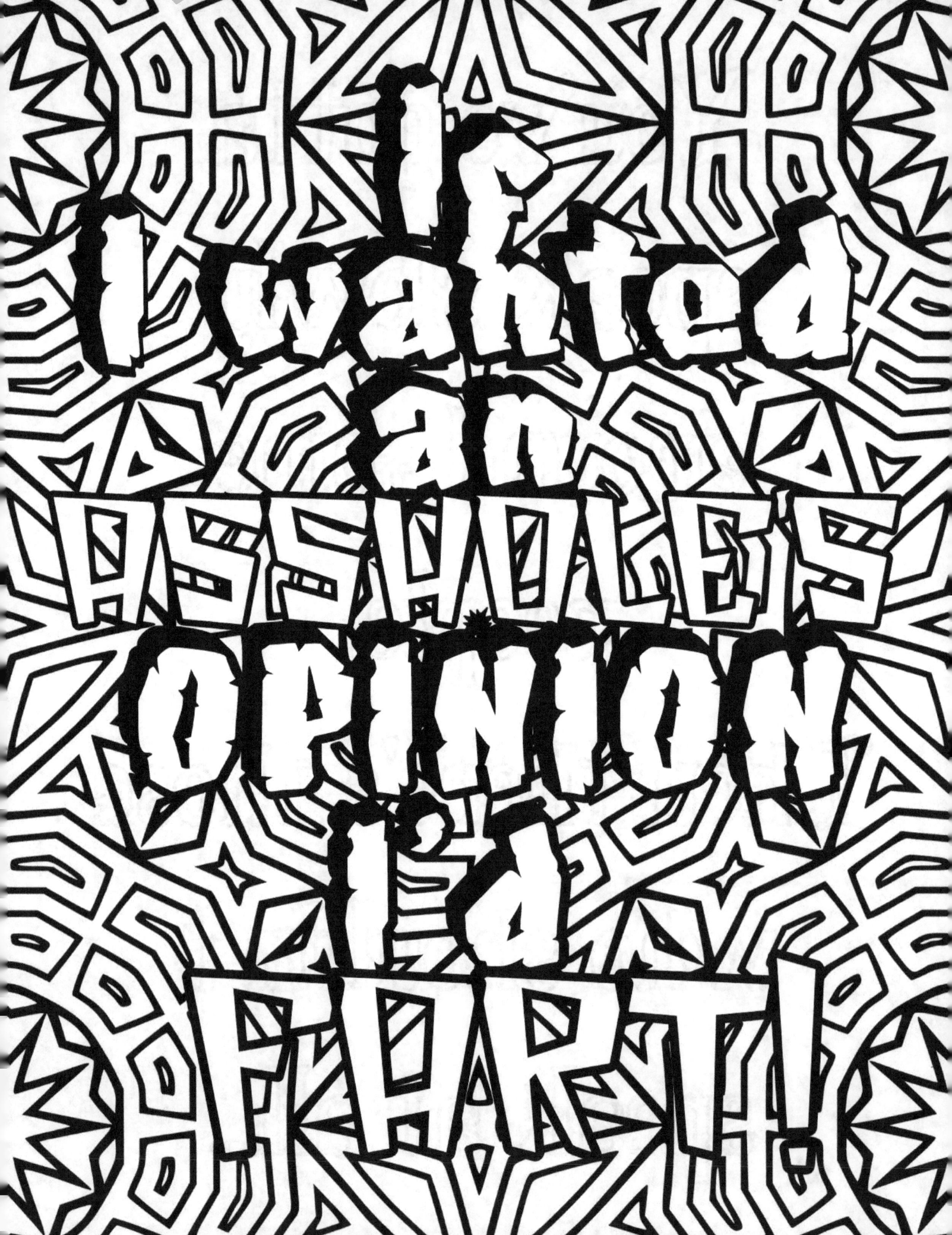

Basically, shut up AND go away! Or put another way...

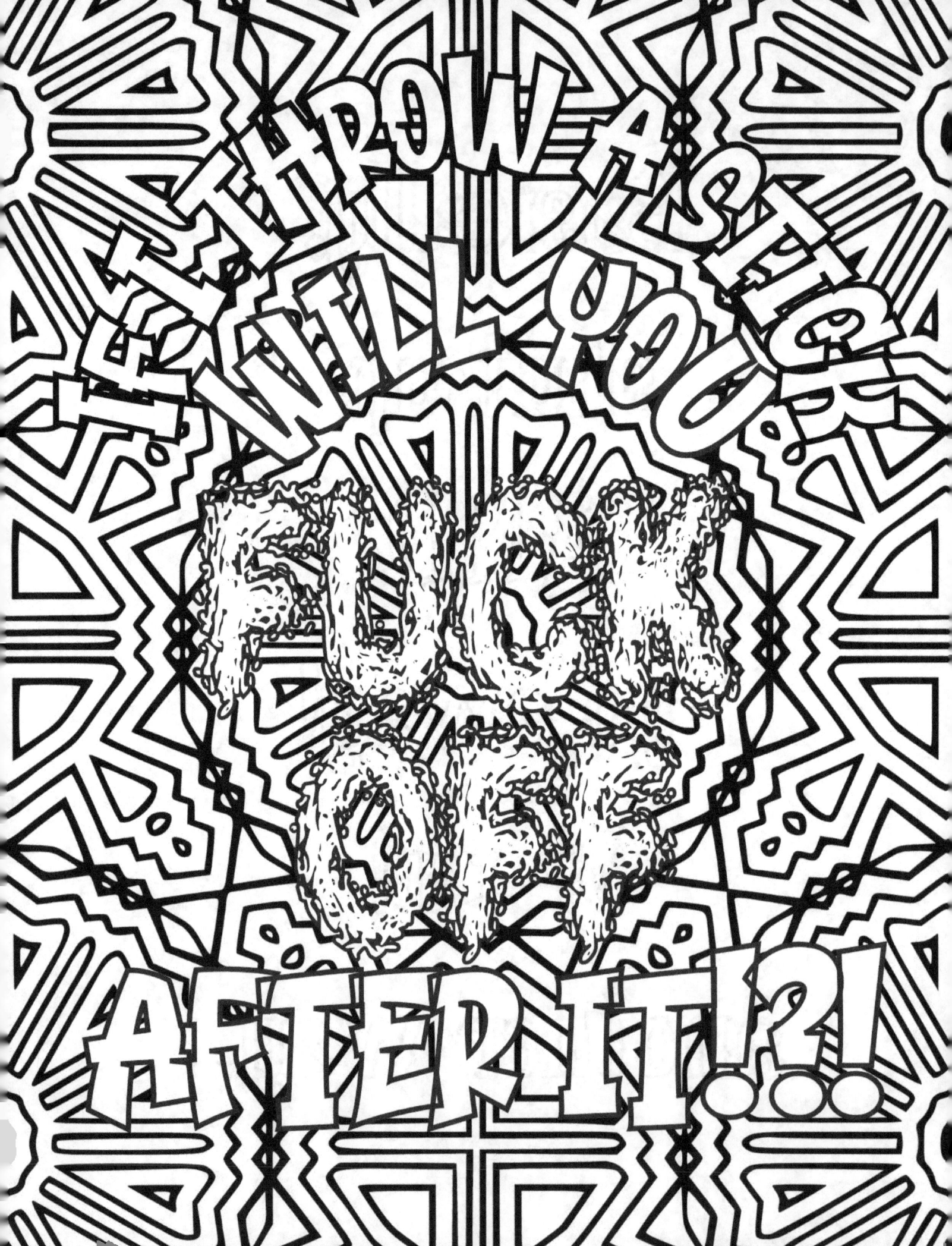

That's a good doggy, you go and play... in traffic. Time to get nasty and dirty.

Now that's one nasty bitch! But don't forget there's some nasty fellas out there, too!

That's beyond nasty, that's fucking disgusting! Now it's time for a good yell!

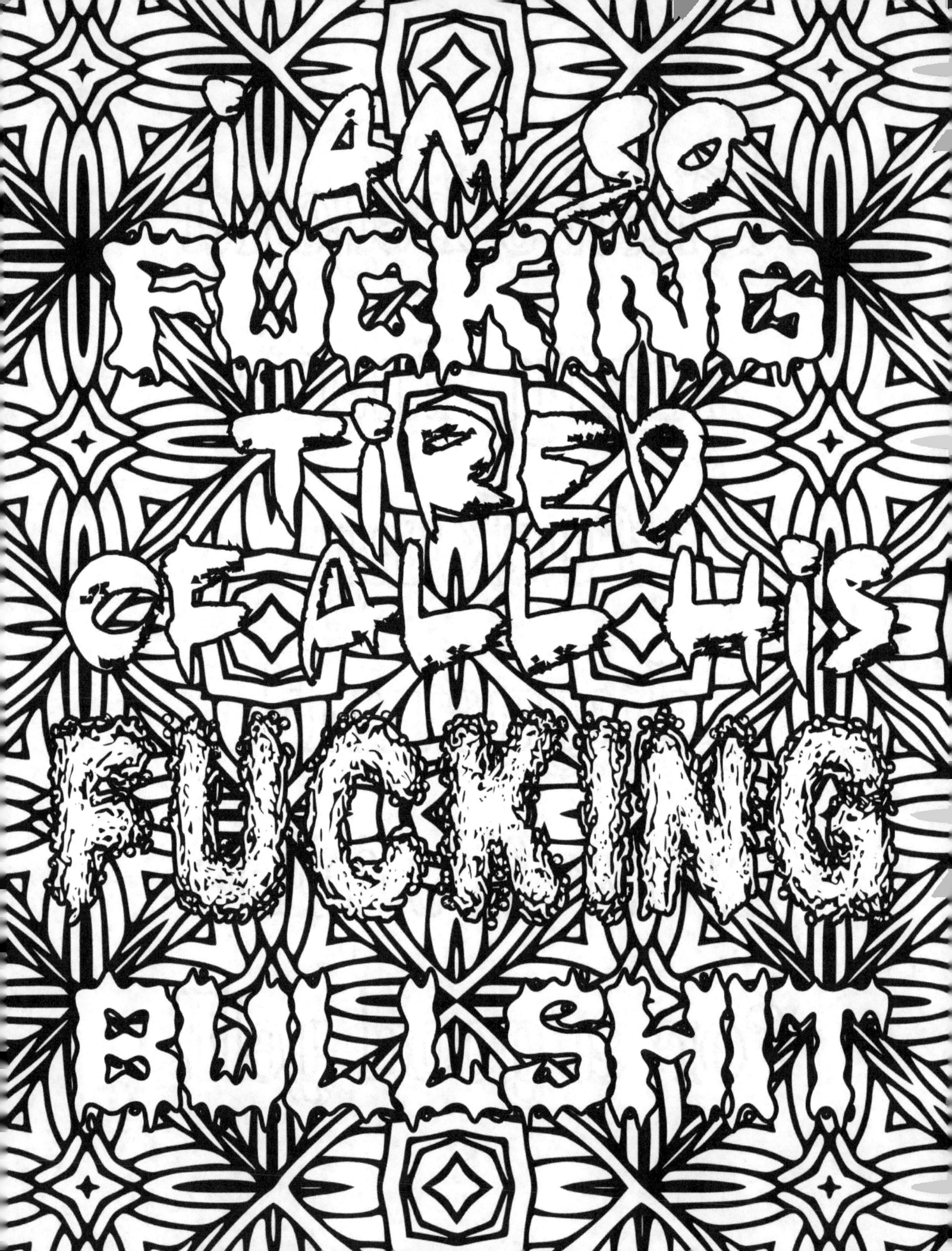

Sometimes, you've got to say it out loud. Or color it. Whatever works. Now, let's be honest...

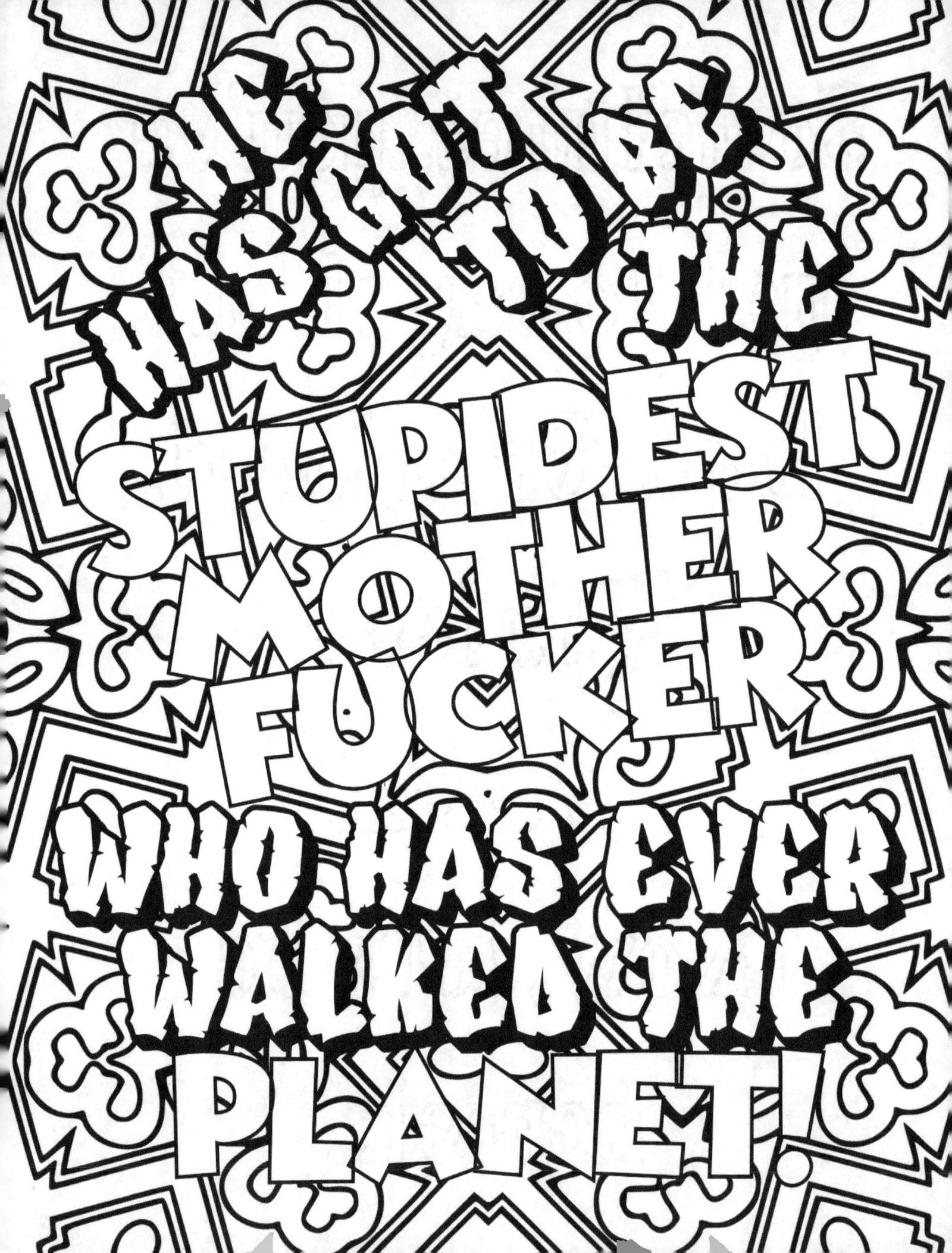

Honesty IS the best policy. This next one, is for the ladies, because some men are pure sleaze!

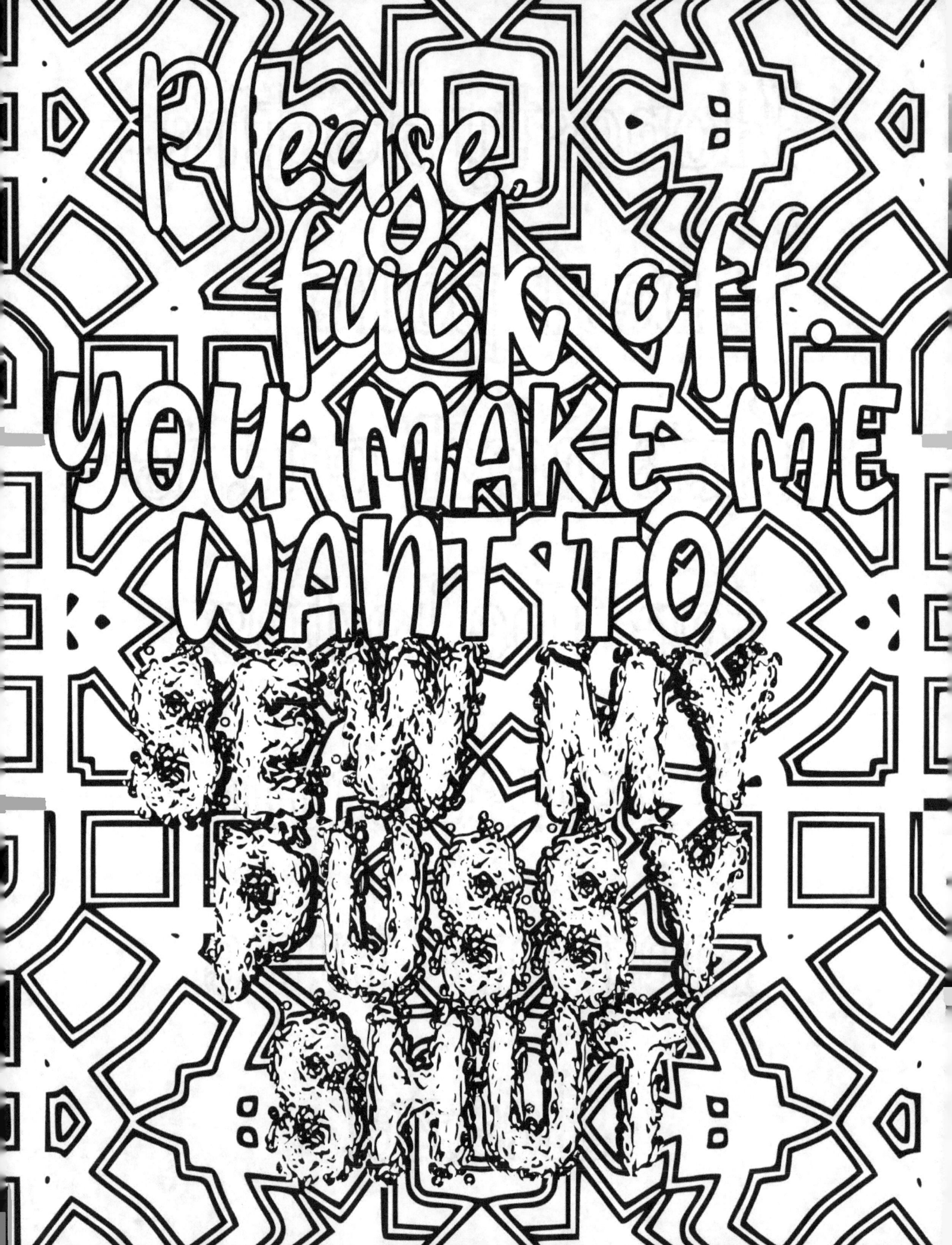

No mixed
messages there!
Damn that's
harsh!
And now the end,
the final truth...

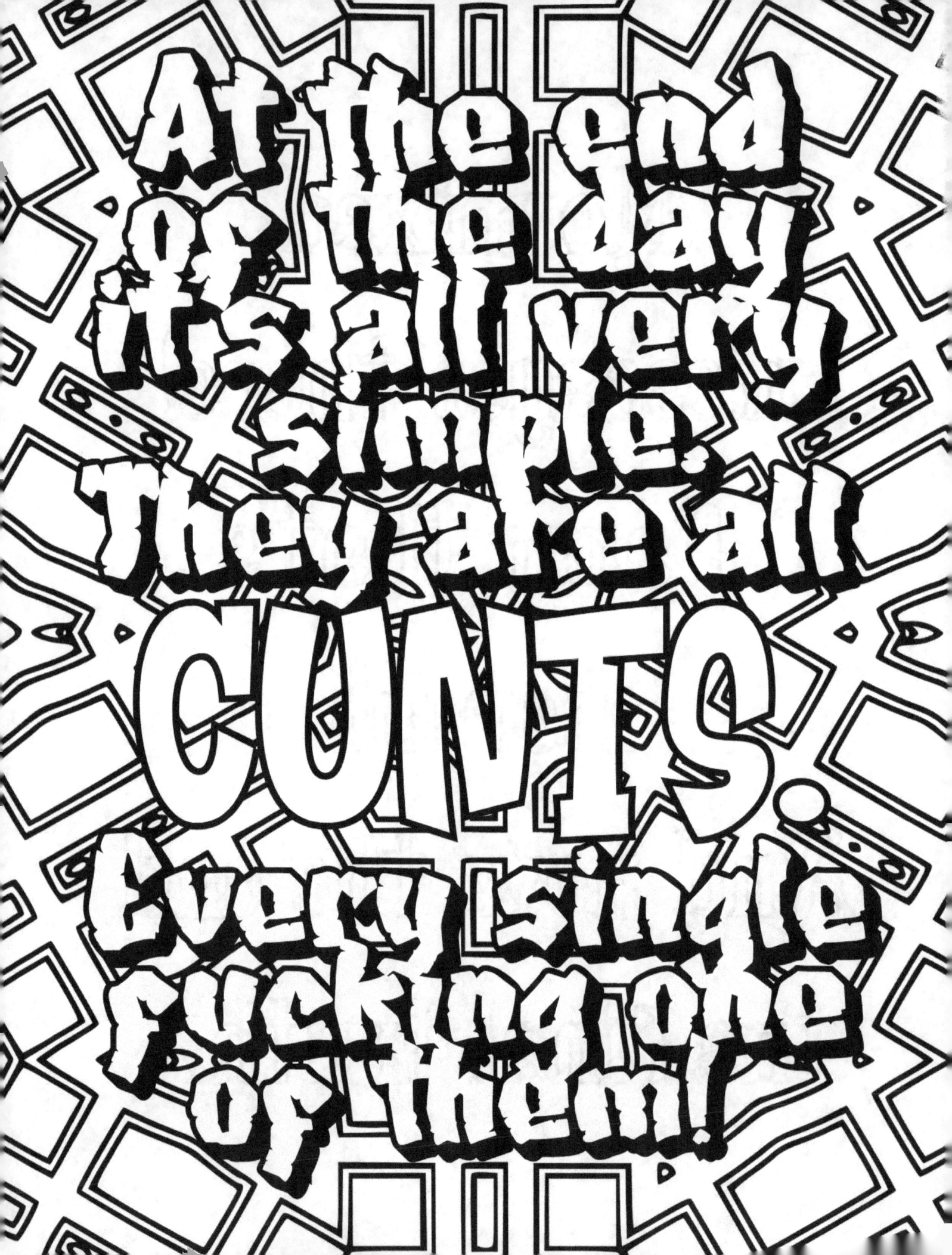

Feel better, yet?
No?!
Then buy another fucking coloring book and do it again!